Acol-ite's Quiz provides easily grasped, light-hearted and thorough instruction on the Acol system of bidding. Designed for use by bridge teachers as a class text, it can easily be used by a student on his own or in competition with others.

There are six sections to the book covering different aspects of bidding. Each has a summary of the relevant rules; thirty exercises, with answers that analyse why a particular bid should be chosen and a series of questions and answers that form a 'Competition Quiz'. Used competitively points are awarded for both the correct bid *and* the correct reason for the choice, and the game against another player can be judged won or lost and progress estimated against a table provided.

D1458370

ACOL-ITE'S QUIZ

Including the Basic Rules of the Acol System,
Quiz Exercises and Competition Quizzes

RHODA LEDERER

FOURTH EDITION

London
UNWIN PAPERBACKS
Boston   Sydney

First published in Great Britain by George Allen & Unwin
1970
First published in Unwin Paperbacks (Second Edition) 1978
Third Edition 1982
Fourth Edition 1985

This book is copyright under the Berne Convention.
No reproduction without permission. All rights reserved.

UNWIN® PAPERBACKS,
40 Museum Street, London, WCIA 1LU, UK

Unwin Paperbacks,
Park Lane, Hemel Hempstead, Herts HP2 4TE, UK

George Allen & Unwin Australia Pty Ltd,
8 Napier Street, North Sydney, NSW 2060, Australia

© George Allen & Unwin (Publishers) Ltd, 1970, 1978, 1982
1985

British Library Cataloguing in Publication Data

Lederer, Rhoda
    Acol-ites quiz.
1.   Contract bridge—Problems, exercises etc.
I.   Title
795.4′152   GV1282.3
ISBN 0-04-793058-6

Printed in Great Britain by
Hazell Watson & Viney Ltd
Aylesbury, Bucks

Contents

FOREWORD

There are six sections in this book, each of which opens with a summary of the rules covering the particular aspect of bidding being considered. These summaries are not intended as a complete explanation of the Acol System which should, of course, be learned from the main text-book, *All About Acol* or in a more elementary form from *The A.B.C. of Contract Bridge*. They will, however, give the reader the main points with which he should be familiar, either as a learner, prospective Acol player, or an Acol player who wants to make sure his bidding is on the right lines.

After each summary comes a series of exercises, each answer being accompanied by an analysis of why a particular bid should be chosen. For instance, a bid may be recommended because it is the only one to express the strength, weakness, or 'shape' of the hand, or the choice of possible alternatives may be conditioned by the need to allow for a sensible rebid on the next round of the auction. You will find that all the most common situations as well as many far less common and even rare ones, have been covered. Amongst the former are examples of the use of 'Directional Asking Bids' and 'Fourth Suit Forcing', mysteries still to many who would regard themselves as competent bidders. If you want to work through these exercises with a friend or 'opponent' it may add to the interest of your study—take it in turns to answer and keep a record of your hits and misses.

Next in each section comes a further series headed 'Competition Quiz'. These questions can, of course, be worked on your own, or they can be used with advantage by bridge teachers for their students, though they are intended primarily as an amusing and instructive game for two people.

Before we come to the method of using the Competition Quizzes as a game, there are one or two points I should like to make. Firstly, remember that, in the ranks of the experts and tournament players, many variations, complications, and partnership 'gadgets', not to mention different interpretations of various bidding sequences, exist. The embryo or club player need not concern himself with these. The examples throughout this book echo the basic system as set out in *All About Acol* and, if you stick to these, you should find yourself able to play comfortably in any company with the minimum difficulty and maximum efficiency.

Secondly, a complete section has been devoted to the development of sequences starting with a no-trump bid, the reason for which is that their inclusion in the other sections would have made these unwieldy. Responses and rebids following a no-trump opening have quite different rules which can be much more clearly covered on their own.

Lastly, the importance of reading the question carefully can't be too highly stressed. If details such as whether or not you are vulnerable, whether or not you are the dealer, or whether another player has opened the bidding or intervened are given, it is because they are relevant to the answer. Don't make mistakes simply through failure to notice these important details.

COMPETITION QUIZ

As a game between two people, each in turn should answer a complete set of questions as instructed at the head of that quiz. Points are awarded, both for finding the correct bid and for giving the correct reason for this choice, and the game, of course, consists of trying to gain more points on your set of questions than your opponent.

If you fail to give the correct bid you can't thereafter score points for giving the correct reason! But if your bid is right you can earn further points by knowing why you made it. It is more than possible to make the right bid for the wrong reason, or even to make what is no more than a lucky guess and hit the jackpot. A good Acol player must, however, know why he is making any particular bid—a lucky guess won't ensure the right action at the bridge table or in a slightly different set of circumstances.

Your wording for your reasons will inevitably differ from that in the quiz answers, but it should not be difficult to judge whether it is basically correct. For example, if the required rebid is 2 N.T. and the printed reason is that a hand of 16+ to 18 points justifies this bid, you clearly know what you are about if you have said that it is too strong for a rebid of 1 N.T. and not strong enough for 3 N.T. In other words, you know why you are bidding 2 N.T., and should score your extra points.

In some instances you will find that you are asked for two bids and, therefore, two reasons, on one quiz hand, with half the available points awarded for each bid and reason. These are divided equally between the **A** and **B** sets of questions to make fair competition.

If you prefer to go through these competition quizzes without an opponent, you should still keep a record of the points you have gained. You could score a maximum of 180 points on each of the **A** and **B** sets, and double that, of course, if you have done both sets on your own. Whether or not you have won or lost to an opponent, have fun grading your ability as an Acol bidder from the table below.

Maximum points available on **A** and **B** questions in each section separately: Bidding ... 72 pts., Reasons ... 108 pts., Total ... 180 pts.

Score:

170-180 pts.	Only two mistakes in 36 problems—your partners are lucky to play with you—only don't let it go to your head.
140-169 pts.	Still reasonably good for a student, but it allows for you to make up to six mistakes in thirty-six bids, too many to be regarded as really efficient.
90-139 pts.	Allowing for lucky guesses, a fair score for a learner, but the lower end of the range means a wrong bid as often as a right one—you're not yet a sound Acol bidder.
Below 90 pts.	Don't be too surprised if you're still looking for people willing to play with you!

R. L.

OPENING BIDS
The Basic Rules

THE first requirement of a dealer's or second-in-hand one-level opening bid is that it should contain a sensible rebid, the reason for which is that partner's change-of-suit response is a one-round force. As third or fourth hand, priority may be given to consideration of whether or not it is expedient to open, either to obstruct or to direct partner's lead, as once partner has passed originally, a change-of-suit response from him is no longer forcing.

An opening bid should aim at expressing as much of the hand as possible—clarification will come at the rebid, if any. But the strongest bid for which the hand qualifies should always be chosen. Thus a one-level suit bid denies the ability to open at the two-level, and a Strong Two opening denies the ability to open 2♣. Even a 2♣ opening denies a hand suitable for an immediate 4 N.T. or five of a major.

1. *Suit Opening Bids at the One-level:*

9-11 pts.	Tactical light opening bids with a six-card suit or two five-card suits as long as these provide a safe rebid.
12 or more pts.	Five-card suit, a five and a four-card suit, or two four-card suits, as long as these provide a sensible rebid.
Up to 20 pts.	Except if fitted for a no-trump opening, and if not suitable for a Strong Two or 2♣ bid, should be opened at the one-level and excess strength shown by a strong rebid.
20 or more pts.	Almost always qualify for better than a one-bid. Hands of 4-4-4-1 pattern with no playing strength by way of suit length are possible exceptions.
4-4-4-1 "shape"	Because of lack of trump length, minimum count should be 13 pts. Open one of the suit below the singleton except when the singleton is clubs, when open 1♡. If only two of the three suits are 'biddable', treat as a two-suiter (see next page).

Two four-card suits | Unless suitable for a no-trump opening bid, with adjacent suits bid higher-ranking first, except with ♣ and ♠, when bid ♣ first. With ♠ and ◇ + ♡ support, ♠ first: with ♠ and ◇ + ♣ support, bid ◇ first: with ♡ and ♣ + ◇ support, ♡ first: with ♡ and ♣ + ♠ support, ♣ first.

1♣ & 1◇ | 'Prepared' minor suit openings are admissible when the hand otherwise contains no sensible rebid. The minor so bid should contain at least three cards to one of the three top honours. If both qualify, bid 1♣.

2. No Trump Opening Bids:

1 N.T. Weak (12-14 pts.) | This is the prescribed strength for a non-vulnerable opening 1 N.T. Preferably evenly-balanced hand with a guard in all suits. A five-card suit is not prohibited.

1 N.T. Strong (15-17 pts) | The prescribed strength when vulnerable, of the same type as the above, except with extra honour count. Highly unlikely to contain a five-card major as this could be bid at the one-level.

Note: The above is known as 'variable no-trump', but the opening strength is optional and based on partnership agreement. 'Weak throughout', 'Strong throughout', or other variations are permitted as long as these are announced to the opponents and there is no more than a 3-point spread (12-14, 13-15, etc).

2 N.T. (20-22 pts) | The same values at any score. Should include a stop in all suits. A balanced hand is recommended though a five-card suit, particularly a minor, is not prohibited.

23-24 pts | These values are shown by an opening bid of 2♣ followed by a rebid of 2 N.T.

25 or more pts | Again, if in a no-trump type hand, these values are shown by an opening bid of 2♣, and this is followed by a rebid of 3 N.T.

3 N.T. | A tactical opening bid based on a long and solid minor suit. Need not concern the learner at this stage.

4 N.T. | Conventional, showing interest *only* in partner's ace-holding, if any. The conventional responses are, with no ace, 5♣: with ◇A, ♡A, ♠A, cue-bid five of the ace-suit: with ♣A, bid 6♣, and with two aces bid 5 N.T.

3. *Strong Two Opening Bids:*

2◇, 2♡,   a) Single-suited hands containing not less than eight
2♠   playing tricks at the suit named.

b) Powerful two-suiters likely to develop eight tricks if the best fit is found.

c) Powerful hands lacking the five Quick Tricks which are needed for a 2♣ opening, but on which there is a danger that the balance of the points may be so divided that a one-level opening may be passed out when little support is needed for a successful game contract. Strong Two openings are forcing for one round, the negative response being 2 N.T.
The emphasis is on playing tricks—do NOT count points for this bid.

4. *2♣ Opening Bids:*

23-24 pts.   Powerful no-trump type hands, shown by a rebid of 2 N.T. The only 2♣ opening which may be passed below game-level.

25+ pts.   Even more powerful no-trump type hands, 2♣ followed by 3 N.T. rebid.

2♣ with   A powerful game-going hand with a minimum of five
a suit   quick tricks and playing strength by way of a good
rebid   trump suit or suits. The suit rebid makes the sequence forcing to game. Count quick tricks, NOT points.

There are two negative responses available, first 2◇, and then 2 N.T. if no more constructive bid can next be found.

5. *Pre-emptive Opening Bids:*

3-level   Hands based on one very long suit, worthless in
or more   defence and containing less than 1½ honour tricks or, generally, four cards in any unbid major.

3 N.T.   See under No. 2 on page 10.

4-level   Long strong major suit and not more than two
in   defensive tricks. Partner is not expected to respond
majors   if he has already passed or, if not yet having had a chance to bid, to make a slam try on less than two aces.

5-level   Both four and five-level opening bids in the minors
in   are purely pre-emptive, based on very long suits and
minors   with no foreseeable defence against the majors.

6. *Conventional High Level Suit Openings:*

5-level in ♡ or ♠	Requests responder to bid the Little Slam with *either* the ace *or* the king of the suit opened, even if the honour card is a singleton, and to bid the Grand Slam if holding both the ace and king. *No* other honour holdings will be of any interest to opener.
6-level in ♡ or ♠	Can be used when, for a Grand Slam, opener is missing only the ace *or* king of his trump suit. Responder should raise to the Grand Slam if holding either, even if singleton.
6-level in ♣ or ◇	Can be used as above in the minors, but *not* at the 5-level, as these minor suit openings are used pre-emptively and not conventionally.

Section 1
OPENING BIDS
Exercises

No. 1   ♠ A Q J 9 6 2   As dealer at any score, what action
          ♡ 9 5   would you take?
          ◇ 8
          ♣ K 10 9 5

Answer : It is always important to consider whether an opening
bid, particularly on a hand which is light in honour strength, is
likely to do more harm than good to your side. But an early
attack almost always pays dividends provided the hand contains a
sensible rebid. As a change-of-suit response from partner is a
one-round force, this is a very necessary consideration.

A six-card suit which can be bid and rebid as a sign-off
constitutes an excellent reason for opening. Not only will you
have gone into the attack early, but you will have indicated a
line of defence to partner if, later, you become a defender.

(Bid: 1♠.)

No. 2   ♠ K 10 8 6 5   As dealer with the score Game All,
          ♡ A K Q J 9   what action would you take on this
          ◇ 9 3   hand?
          ♣ 4

Answer : With 13 pts. and two five-card majors you would always
open the bidding, whatever your position at the table and whatever
the score.

Here your choice is simple—with two equal and adjacent suits
the rule is to open one of the higher-ranking first, which gives you
a safe rebid in the other. It doesn't matter that the hearts are so
much stronger—they will come in useful anyway. The important
point is to give yourself the best chance to tell your partner that
you have a biddable spade suit and, if the auction comes round to
you again, a biddable heart suit too. Unless he has strong ideas
of his own, he will then be in a position to let you play in the one
which fits his hand best.

(Bid: 1♠.)

No. 3   ♠ A Q 10 7   As dealer, whatever the score, what
       ♥ K J 8   opening bid would you make on this
       ♦ 3 2   hand?
       ♣ A Q 10 7

Answer : The rules for your choice between two four-card suits
are the same as for five-card suits. With equal and adjacent suits
bid the higher-ranking first. With non-adjacent suits other con-
siderations may come into it, as we shall see later.

Meanwhile here's another rule—with equal lengthed *black* suits
in a hand qualifying for no better than a one-bid, *bid the clubs
first*. This has two advantages; firstly, having started with 1♣ you
have a simple rebid of 1♠ if partner responds in a red suit and,
secondly, as the auction develops, he will be able to tell that
you have at least as many clubs as spades, if not more. As you
should always try to bid a longer suit before a shorter, and as a
suit is not *re*biddable if it is of less than five-card length, if you
open 1♣ and subsequently bid and rebid spades, showing that
the second suit is rebiddable, or of at least five-cards, then your
hand must contain at least ten black cards. Here you could not
rebid either black suit.

(Bid: 1♣.)

No. 4   ♠ K 10 8 6 5   This is the same hand as No. 2
       ♥ 9 3   except that the red suits have chang-
       ♦ A K Q J 9   ed places. What dealer's opening
       ♣ 4   bid, if any, would you make?

Answer : This time your suits are not adjacent, and you must
give careful thought to the future of the auction. If you open 1♦
and responder bids 1♥, all is well as you rebid 1♠, which is
neither forcing nor unduly encouraging. But if responder bids 2♣
over 1♦, you would have to show your spades at the two-level,
which is reserved for much stronger hands. This would mean
falling back on a rebid of 2♦, for ever concealing your five-card
major.

If, however, you open 1♠, you can safely rebid 2♦ over a
response of 2♣, and if the response to 1♠ is 2♥, you rebid 2♠,
at least not having concealed your major suit. Certainly you may
have to bid a little untruthfully, but all kinds of things may have
happened to the auction before you have to bid a second time.

(Bid: 1♠.)

No. 5   ♠ A Q 9 5   Would you open on this hand and,
       ♡ 6   if so, what would you bid? Would
       ◇ K Q 8 2   it make any difference if your dia-
       ♣ K J 8 3   monds were changed to ◇Q-10-8-2?

Answer: The first rule for 4-4-4-1 hands with three biddable suits
is to open one of the suit below the singleton, so you bid 1◇.
This is, of course, bearing in mind the need for a sensible rebid,
as if partner responds 1♡ you can bid 1♠, and if he responds 2♣
you can raise him, knowing a spade fit has not been missed.

With the ◇K missing your hand would be worth only 12 pts.,
and though there are many 'shapes' on which this would be more
than ample, 4-4-4-1 isn't one of them. There is no playing
strength by way of a long suit so that if you are forced to ruff
hearts early on, the hand may well fall to pieces. 4-4-4-1 hands
should contain a minimum of 13 pts., and preferably more.

(Bids: 1◇ and No Bid.)

No. 6   ♠ A Q 9 5   This is the same hand as No. 5
       ♡ K J 8 3   except that the clubs have become
       ◇ K Q 8 2   hearts. What difference, if any, would
       ♣ 6   this make to your correct opening
                        bid?

Answer : The choice of opening bid must frequently be based on
thought for the future. If you open 1♠, which is now technically
'the suit below the singleton', you will be able to do no better
than guess what to bid next if partner responds 2♣. Whichever
you choose, you may miss a good fit in the other.

Assuming that partner will normally elect to make a spade
response if he can do so, if you open 1♡ you make it easy for
him to respond 1♠ and, if he still bids 2♣, you are pretty sure
no spade fit has been missed, so can rebid 2◇ quite happily. If
he responds 2◇ or raises hearts, you've found the fit anyway.

So the rule set out in No. 5 now has an addition. Open one of
the suit below the singleton except when the singleton is in clubs,
when open 1♡.

(Bid: 1♡.)

No. 7   ♠ 7   What opening bid would you make
        ♡ 6 5 4 3   on this 4-4-4-1 hand?
        ◇ A Q 9 5
        ♣ A K 9 2

Answer : This time only two of the three four-card suits can really be considered 'biddable' in a 13-pt. hand. In other words, the heart suit is not one you want to suggest as the trump suit unless partner can bid it, when you would, of course, support him.

Treating this hand as a minor two-suiter, therefore, you simply open 1◇, the higher-ranking. If partner responds 1♠ you can rebid 2♣ with a clear conscience, and if instead he responds 1♡, the least you can do is to raise him to 3♡. A direct raise to 4♡ would be stretching things too far, as responder might have a mere 6 pts. for his one-level response. If he has more, he should be capable of taking the hint!

(Bid : 1 ◇.)

No. 8   ♠ A J 9   At Love All, what opening bid
        ♡ K J 9 8   would you make?
        ◇ K 8 4
        ♣ J 10 8

Answer : This depends on the agreed strength of your no-trump opening, which is one of the optional features of the Acol System. You can agree 'weak throughout', which means 12-14 pts. at any score, 'strong throughout', which means 15-17 pts. at any score, or 'variable', which means weak when not vulnerable and strong when vulnerable. You will find that there are also other variations in use, particularly in the tournament world.

In these quizzes we shall work on 'variable', so be sure to learn what this means now. In this way you will learn to handle both 'weak' and 'strong', and can decide which you prefer.

1 N.T. is the perfect opening bid on this hand when using the weak variety. It is evenly-balanced, contains 13½ pts. (10's count ½ pt. in no-trump bidding) and has 'something in everything'.

(Bid : 1 N.T.)

No. 9 ♠ K J 8   At Game All, using a variable no-
       ♡ K J 9 8   trump, what opening bid would you
       ◇ A 9 8   make on this hand?
       ♣ J 6 2

Answer :   Using a weak no-trump this would be the perfect bid
on this hand but you are not strong enough for a 15-17 pt. no-
trump opening—it's important not to promise a minimum of 15 pts.
when you have, in fact, only 13. Nor are you strong enough to
open 1♡, your four-card suit, as this could well put you into
difficulties for a truthful rebid. This is one of the rare occasions
when you must fall back on a 'prepared' minor suit opening.

  Don't bid 1♣, as even for a 'prepared' bid there are specific
requirements—the suit should contain at least three cards, one of
which is one of the three top honours. Your clubs don't qualify,
so you must open 1◇.

                                     (Bid: 1◇.)

No. 10 ♣ A J 10 8   At Game All, what opening bid
       ♡ K J 10 7   would you make on this hand?
       ◇ A J
       ♣ A 7 4

Answer :   Whatever the score you are too strong to open 1 N.T.
on this hand, as even a strong no-trump promises *not more* than
17 pts. Nor is this the moment for a 'prepared' 1♣, even though
the suit qualifies, so think again! *Never* make a prepared bid on
a hand with a sensible alternative.

  1♠, the higher-ranking of equal and adjacent suits, would be
a lesser evil than 1♣, but there is an even better bid available.
This is a strong hand admirably suited to play in no-trumps if
partner responds in a minor suit, but splendidly equipped for a
game in either major if partner has a four-card fit. On the grounds
that he will respond in spades if he can, make it easy for him.
Open 1♡ and rebid 3 N.T. if he bids 2♣ or 2◇. If he responds
1♠, however, raise to 4 ♠ (cf. Hand No. 7). In this way you won't
miss a heart fit either.

                                     (Bid: 1♡.)

No. 11 ♠ Q 8 6 4
♥ A Q 9 3
♦ A Q 9 8 5
♣ —

As dealer, what opening bid would you make on this hand?

Answer : The rules for opening suit bids are quite clear—the longer suit before the shorter, the higher-ranking before the lower, and the stronger before the weaker. But these, as we have already seen, must give way to the need to consider an honest rebid.

The rule covering this hand is, of course, the first, so you open 1♢, knowing that you can support partner strongly if he responds in either major, and that your diamonds are good enough to *re*bid if he responds in clubs. This should be your guide before you decide, as well you might, to treat this hand as you would do a 4-4-4-1 distribution with a singleton club, on which you would open 1♡. Take some of your diamond honour strength out into your spades, and you would not want to put yourself into the position of having to rebid the diamonds. Only then would you open 1♡ and risk subsequent preference to a suit you don't actually prefer.

(Bid: 1♢.)

No. 12 ♠ A J 9 7
♥ K 8 7
♦ A Q 6 2
♣ 5 3

As dealer at Game All, what opening bid would you make on this hand?

Answer : You must choose, of course, between your two four-card suits, and you can't get yourself off the hook of this decision by bidding 1 N.T. for which you are too weak. Nor, incidentally, would the hand make a good weak no-trump opening containing, as it does, a worthless doubleton and a sensible alternative bid.

In this case you are able to keep to the rule about opening the higher-ranking suit before the lower, that is, you open 1♠. Working out the likely development of the auction, you can see that this leaves you a sensible rebid. If partner responds 2♣ you can safely rebid 2♢, and if he responds either 2♢ or 2♡, you can raise. If you make the mistake of opening 1♢ you have no problem if the response is 1♡, but you have nothing sensible to say if the response is 2♣.

(Bid: 1♠.)

No. 13 ♠ A J 9 7   As dealer at Game All, what open-
       ♡ 5 3   ing bid would you make on this
       ◇ A Q 6 2   hand?
       ♣ K 8 7

Answer : This is the same hand as No. 12 except that the hearts and clubs have changed places, though this makes all the difference.

On No. 12 you opened 1♠ because you realised that this was the bid best calculated to make your rebid simple. This time, if you open 1♠ and partner bids 2♣ you can happily rebid 2◇, but you are in difficulties if, instead, he bids 2♡. With one more point —say the ♣J—you could bid 2 N.T. but as it is, not only were you under strength for a strong no-trump opening, but you are under strength for a 2 N.T. rebid. Open 1◇, which gives you a sensible rebid of 1♠ to a response of 1♡, or a raise in clubs to a response of 2♣. If partner can't himself produce a further bid, you don't want to be in a high-level contract on a somewhat flat 14 pts.

(Bid: 1◇.)

No. 14 ♠ 5 3   As dealer at Game All, what open-
       ♡ A J 9 7   ing bid would you make on this
       ◇ K 8 7   hand?
       ♣ A Q 6 2

Answer : Note that here, as well as in Nos. 12 and 13, you were vulnerable which means that, using a variable no-trump, you had no option but to pick one of your suits for your opening bid. As before, work out the probable development of the auction to help you to decide between your alternatives of 1♣ and 1♡.

If you open 1♣ and the response is 1♠, what are you to bid next? Your only course would be to fall back on 1 N.T. which might well mean missing a far better contract. If, however, you open 1♡, you can rebid 2♣ in reply to partner's 1♠, or raise him if he bids 2◇.

You will see from these examples that, with two four-card suits, and when your count prohibits a 1 N.T. opening, your choice may be conditioned by the suit for which you have support if partner bids it.

(Bid: 1♡.)

No. 15 ♠ A Q 6
   ♡ K 10 9 5
   ◇ K 8 6
   ♣ K 9 2

As dealer, what vulnerable opening bid would you make on this hand, and would it make any difference if you were not vulnerable?

Answer : This is an excellent hand for a strong, i.e. vulnerable, 1 N.T. opening. It tells partner everything in one bid, leaving you no problem as to a rebid.

Not vulnerable, you are too strong for 1 N.T., and there is nothing whatsoever against opening 1♡, your four-card suit. You have a stop in each suit and the right count for a rebid of 2 N.T. if partner respond 2♣ or 2◇, or 1 N.T. if he bids 1♠.

Compare this hand with No. 9 on which you had to fall back on a 'prepared' opening. This was because, with only 14 pts., you were not strong enough to rebid no-trumps at the two-level.

(Bids: 1 N.T. and 1♡.)

No. 16 ♠ K J 9 2
   ♡ K 8 6 5 3
   ◇ A Q 7
   ♣ 6

As dealer, whatever the score, would you open on this hand and, if so, what would you bid?

Answer : Yes, with two biddable major suits and 13 pts., you must open, so it only remains to consider which of the rules apply or whether it might be wiser to 'bend' one of them a bit.

If you stick to the rule of bidding your longer suit, hearts, first, you cannot possibly 'reverse' into 2♠ if partner responds 2♣, and nor do you really want to repeat a suit which is quite as weak and straggly as your hearts. Whether you choose to open 1♡ and rebid 2♡, or open 1♠ and rebid 2♡ is something of a matter of style. But on balance I think it wiser to open 1♠, the only risk you run being that later in the auction partner may give you preference to this suit, which you don't really prefer. Compare No. 11 which illustrates a somewhat similar point.

(Bid: 1♠.)

No. 17 ♠ A K J 7   What opening bid would you make
        ♡ A Q J 5 3   on this hand?
        ◇ K 7
        ♣ 8 4

Answer : This is a very different proposition from No. 16. Here
you have two good biddable suits and—even more important—
a strong honour count. This means that you can afford to keep to
the rule of opening the longer suit before the shorter, so you bid
1♡. You will then be able to use a forcing 'reverse' into 2♠ if
partner responds in either minor.

You will learn more about 'reversing' in Section 4 but, in the
meantime, look back to No. 16 and consider your plight if, having
decided to open 1♡, partner had responded 2♣ and you had
rebid 2♠. Your partner would understand this as forcing and
would probably have raised to 3♠ or put you back to 3♡—and
you wouldn't like it at all! With the hand above, you would have
no such reservations.

(Bid: 1♡.)

No. 18 ♠ 7   At game to your opponents you deal
        ♡ A Q 8 6 5 4 3   yourself this hand. Would you bid
        ◇ 9   and, if so, what?
        ♣ 9 7 6 4

Answer : This is an ideal hand for an opening pre-emptive bid
of 3♡, the idea of which it to disrupt your opponents' bidding to
the fullest possible extent.

Unfortunately your partner has not yet had a chance to bid,
so he may be the one in difficulties, from which you will realise
that the best position for a pre-emptive opening is third-in-hand
after two passes. But in Section 2 you will learn how responder,
if he has a strong hand, should cope. Meanwhile, you will have
warned him of the character of your hand as well as forcing your
opponents, if they want to come into the bidding, to start at what
may be an uncomfortably high level. You have robbed them of
bidding space, which may make it impossible for them to discover
their own best contract.

(Bid: 3♡.)

No. 19 ♠ 9 7 6 4
       ♡ A Q 8 6 5 4 3
       ◇ 9
       ♣ 7

At game to your opponents, what dealer's opening bid would you make, and would it make any difference if you were third-in-hand after two passes?

Answer : This is the same hand as No. 18 except that the black suits have changed places. Now you have wonderful 'shape' and excellent spade support if partner, who has not yet had a chance to bid, is contemplating opening in spades. You don't want to talk him out of this so, as dealer, it is better to pass and bide your time.

Once partner has passed, showing that he lacks the values for an opening bid, there is less need to worry about talking him out of bidding spades. By opening 3♡ you might, of course, talk your opponents out of bidding spades, but it looks more as though they will be strong in the minors, if anything. It's worth the risk, so open 3♡.

(Bids: No Bid and 3♡.)

No. 20 ♠ 9 7
       ♡ A Q J 10 6 5 4 2
       ◇ A
       ♣ 8 4

As dealer, what opening bid would you make, and would the score, or your position at the table, make any difference?

Answer : Taking the second part of the question first, no, neither the score nor your position at the table would make any difference to the fact that you have a full-scale Acol Strong Two opening in hearts.

There are three classes of Strong Two but the first, of which this is an excellent example, is a hand with eight playing tricks at the suit named. Allowing for any reasonable distribution of the outstanding hearts you have seven winners in the suit which, plus the ◇A, makes eight tricks. Strong Two bids, of course, can be made in spades, hearts, and diamonds, but not in clubs.

Nor do you count points—count playing tricks.

(Bid: 2♡.)

No. 21   ♠ A K Q 9 8   What opening bid would you make
         ♡ 8 4   on this hand?
         ◇ A K J 10 8 7
         ♣ —

Answer :   This is another class of Strong Two opening, a powerful
two-suiter on which you need to make sure of a chance to show
both suits, asking for partner's preference, as even the most slender
support for the one which fits his hand best is likely to produce
game.

Open 2◇, the longer of your two suits, prepared to make a
forcing 'reverse' into 3♠ if partner responds 2 N.T. (cf. Hand No.
17). Partner will then know that you fancy your chances of making
game in 4♠ or 5◇ and that your diamonds are the longer. He will
either raise 3♠ to 4♠ or put you back into diamonds.

(Bid: 2◇.)

No. 22   ♠ A K Q 9 8   What opening bid would you make
         ♡ 8 4   on this hand?
         ◇ —
         ♣ A K 10 9 8 7

Answer :   It is permissible, when the predominating suit is clubs,
to make a 2♣ opening when a little under strength, but this should
be confined to hands on which you really have no alternative.

This hand, though just a trifle weaker than No. 21 (missing the
♣J) is still a powerful two-suiter. Open 2♠ intending to make
your rebid in clubs. If, for example, partner responds to 2♠ with
the negative 2 N.T., make a jump rebid of 4♣, which is forcing.
Partner must either give preference to 4♠ or raise to 5♣, either
of which you should have a good chance of making once the best
fit has been found.

(Bid: 2♠.)

No. 23 ♠ A K 7 2   What opening bid would you make
       ♡ A K J 10 6   on this hand?
       ◇ —
       ♣ K 7 5 4

Answer: Just to make it clear that there are many powerful hands which qualify for no better than a one-level opening, here is an example. You cannot truly tell yourself that it is so constituted that a pass from partner is likely to cost you a missed game, and nor is it vitally urgent for you to ensure yourself a chance to show a second suit.

Content yourself with a bid of 1♡, though being fully prepared to 'reverse' into 2♠ on the next round, if any. Only if partner can bid without being forced in the first place do you want to insist on a game contract, though obviously if he can show any signs of life, you will take strong action.

(Bid: 1♡.)

No. 24 ♠ A K 10 5 4   What opening bid would you make
       ♡ A Q J 10   on this hand?
       ◇ Q 3
       ♣ A 7

Answer: This is an example of the third class of Strong Two opening, a hand which is too strong to risk a bid at the one-level which might be passed out, so open 2♠. This gives you a sure chance to show your hearts on the next round and, in fact, to explore for the best final contract. In the actual event, partner made a 'positive' response—in hearts!—and there was no problem about reaching the heart slam contract.

You don't count honour points when considering a Strong Two opening. You count playing strength, and also take into account the urgency of ensuring a chance to rebid, in order to express the nature of your hand.

(Bid: 2♠.)

No. 25 ♠ A K 6
     ♡ A 10 3
     ◊ K 9 8
     ♣ A K 7 4

Whatever your position at the table, and whatever the score, what opening bid would you make on this hand?

Answer: A hand should always be opened with the strongest bid for which it qualifies, which in this case is 2 N.T., showing 20-22 pts. in a balanced hand. You have, of course, the five quick trick needed for a 2♣ opening, but not the playing strength that this bid also promises.

As an Acol player, each bid you make will promise something and also, by reason of the fact that you made that particular bid, it can also deny the values for an even stronger bid. Just as 1 N.T. promises an agreed honour count, so 2 N.T. promises 20-22 pts., and a 2♣ opening followed by a 2 N.T. rebid promises 23-24 pts. An even strong hand of 25 or more pts. can be shown by a 2♣ opening and a 3 N.T. rebid.

(Bid: 2 N.T.)

No. 26 ♠ A 6 2
     ♡ A K 3
     ◊ 5 4 2
     ♣ A K 4 2

What opening bid would you make on this hand?

Answer: Here you have five quick tricks, but you have nothing approaching 'shape' or 'playing strength'. In fact if partner can't respond under his own steam you may well end up with just the five top tricks you started with.

This is not a hand for a power announcement. Be content with a quiet 1♣ chosen, not for the sake of making a 'prepared' bid, but because with 18 pts. you can afford to open one of your longest suit, whatever it is. If partner can respond at all the future will look much brighter, and you will be able to make a forcing rebid if not a direct jump to game. For example, if partner responds 1 N.T. which, facing 1♣, shows 8-10 pts., you would rebid 3 N.T.

(Bid: 1♣.)

No. 27 ♠ A K 10 8   As dealer, what opening bid would
♥ A Q J 10 9   you make on this hand?
♦ —
♣ A K 7 2

Answer : It wouldn't make any difference whether you were
dealer, second, third, or fourth hand as long as you were the
opening bidder—you have a full-strength opening power house
qualifying for 2♣.

It's easy to see that the rest of the points could be so distributed
that a one-bid could be passed out, and a Strong Two would do
nothing like justice to the hand. You have not counted points on
this hand, but quick tricks and playing strength, and you need
the minimum of help from partner to be sure of at least a game.
The 2♣ opening bid, particularly when it is clarified by a game-
forcing suit rebid of 2♡, will tell him this—the best possible reason
for opening 2♣ and not some lesser bid.

If anyone has taught you that you need 23 points to open 2♣,
forget it. Only bother with counting points if you intend to rebid
in no-trumps.

(Bid: 2♣.)

No. 28 ♠ A Q 7   What opening bid would you make
♥ A J 10 6   on this hand? What difference would
♦ A Q   it make if the ♣Q became the ♣9
♣ A Q 8 5   *or* if the ♡J became the ♡K?

Answer : This is an evenly-balanced collection, obviously fitted
for play in no-trumps, so you start by counting your points, not
quick tricks or playing tricks. Your total is 23½ pts., too strong
for a 2 N.T. opening, so you bid 2♣, intending to rebid 2 N.T. to
show 23-24 pts.

If the hand were missing the ♣Q it would fall within the range
of a 2 N.T. opening bid and if, with the ♣Q where she is, the
♡J became the ♡K, it would still be correct to open 2♣, though
this time with the intention of rebidding 3 N.T. to show 25 or more
honour points.

(Bids : 2♣, 2 N.T., and 2♣.)

No. 29 ♠ A K
      ♥ Q J 10 9 8 7 6 5
      ♦ A K Q
      ♣ —

What opening bid would you make on this hand?

Answer: Believe it or not, this is an actual hand from play, and is a perfect example of a 5♡ opening bid—perfectly safe as long as partner knows his Acol!

All you need to make 6♡ a certainty is either the ace *or* king of the suit in partner's hand, even if it is only a singleton, and if by some miracle he should have both, 7♡ is equally safe. Yet you have only 19 pts. and if partner should turn up with 14 of the outstanding ones, which don't include either the ♡A or ♡K, you will have a hard job to keep him from bidding a slam if you've made the mistake of opening 2♣ or even 2♡.

An opening of 5♡ or 5♠ instructs responder to raise to six if he holds either the ace or king of your suit, even if it is a singleton and, with both, to raise to seven. It also tells him that none of the other cards in the pack are of any interest.

(Bid: 5♡.)

No. 30 ♠ A K Q
      ♥ A K Q
      ♦ K Q J 10 9 8 7
      ♣ —

What opening bid would you make on this hand?

Answer: To end this section, here's another cracking big opening bid, this time a conventional 4 N.T., because partner's exact cards are of supreme importance. If he has the ♢A you want to play in 7♢, but even if he has a Yarborough, you want to play in 6♢.

If you open 2♣ and subsequently bid a 'Blackwood' 4 N.T., a 5♢ reply showing one ace would leave you guessing at to whether it were the vital ♢A or the useless ♣A. Open 4 N.T., which asks for the following responses—with the ♢A, ♡A, or ♠A, five of the ace suit, with the ♣A, 6♣, and with two aces, 5 N.T. With no ace, of course, the response is 5♣, and opener's decision after the initial response must be taken as final.

(Bid: 4 N.T.)

Section 1
OPENING BIDS
Competition Quiz

IN competition against another player, one should answer the three questions in the **A** set, and the other the three questions in the **B** set on each page.

1A. As dealer at Love All, what opening bids would you make?

	1.	2.	3.
♠	Q J 9 6 3	10 6	10 6
♡	K Q 10 7 4	A Q 9 8 6	A Q 9 8 6 4
◇	7	9	9 3
♣	A 3	K 10 9 3 2	K 10 9

Answers:

Bid (2 pts.)   Reason (3 pts.)

1. 1♠   The higher-ranking of equal and adjacent suits, allowing for a safe rebid in the other.

2. No   Had the suits been adjacent you could have consider-
    Bid ed opening in the higher-ranking. As it is, neither suit nor the outside strength warrants an opening bid.

3. 1♡   A six-card suit, which is always *re*biddable, affords a safe sign-off rebid.

1B. As dealer at Love All, what opening bids would you make?

	1.	2.	3.
♠	Q J 9 6 3	10 6	Q J 9 6 3
♡	7	A K J 8 6	7
◇	K Q 10 7 4	A 10 7 4	A 3
♣	A 3	J 8	K Q 10 7 4

Answers:

Bid (2 pts.)   Reason (3 pts.)

1. 1♠   Too good to pass. Open 1♠ intending to rebid 2◇ if partner responds 2♣. If, however, the response is 2♡, you will have to rebid 2♠, as the hand it not good enough to show a new suit at the three-level (a one-round force).

2. 1♡   A full-strength opening hand with a safe rebid in its second suit, even though this is only a four-card one.

3. 1♣   Now the two five-card suits are both black, and the correct opening is 1♣, leaving a safe rebid in spades if partner responds in a red suit.

2A. As dealer at Love All, what opening bids would you make?

1. ♠ K J 9 7 4	2. ♠ A K Q J	3. ♠ K J 9 7 4
♡ A Q J 10 6	♡ K J 9 7 4	♡ 9 6 3
♢ K 7	♢ 9 6 3	♢ 7
♣ 8	♣ 7	♣ A K Q J

Answers:
Bid (2 pts.)   Reason (3 pts.)

1.   1♠   The higher-ranking of equal and adjacent suits. You must not let the heart honours go to your head, as discovering the best suit fit is far more important than the honours bonus.

2.   1♠   In spite of the rule that the longer suit should be bid before the shorter, an opening of 1♡ leaves you no sensible rebid if partner responds 2♣, whereas an opening of 1♠ leaves you a rebid of 2♡. (Note that this is a matter of style—some players would prefer to open 1♡ and rebid hearts unless responder bids spades.)

3.   1♠   If you open 1♣ partner will be entitled to understand from a subsequent spade bid that your clubs are at least as long as, if not longer, than your spades.

2B. As dealer at Love All, what opening bids would you make?

1. ♠ K J 9 7 4	2. ♠ 9 3	3. ♠ 9 6 3
♡ 9 3	♡ K J 9 7 4	♡ K J 9 7 4
♢ 7	♢ 7	♢ 7
♣ A K Q J 10	♣ A K Q J 10	♣ A K Q J

Answers:
Bid (2 pts.)   Reason (3 pts.)

1.   1♣   This is a simple case of two black suits of equal length. Open 1♣ leaving yourself a sensible rebid of 1♠.

2.   1♣   With these two non-adjacent suits you choose to open 1♣ because the suit is good enough to rebid if partner bids 1♠. If he bids 1♢, you rebid 1♡.

3.   1♡   The four-card club suit is not *rebiddable*. Open 1♡ intending to rebid 2♣ over 1♠ or repeat hearts over 2♢.

3A. What opening bids would you make if using a weak no-trump, and what if using a strong no-trump?

1. ♠ A Q 9	2. ♠ A Q 9	3. ♠ A Q 9
♡ K J 6	♡ K 8 6	♡ K J 6
◇ Q 10 7 4	◇ Q 10 9 7 4	◇ Q 10 7
♣ J 6 2	♣ Q 6	♣ K 10 6 2

Answers:

Bids (1 pt. each)   Reasons (1½ pts. each)

1. 1 N.T. if using 'weak' as this leaves you no rebid problems.
   1◇   if using "strong", the hand is not up to standard for 1 N.T. The clubs don't qualify even for a 'prepared' 1♣.

2. 1 N.T. if using 'weak'. A slight compromise, as the hand contains no satisfactory rebid if you open 1◇.
   1◇   which is the only possible alternative to passing.

3. 1♣   if using 'weak'—too strong for 1 N.T.
   1 N.T. if using "strong", for which it is perfectly fitted.

3B. What opening bids would you make if using a weak no-trump, and what if using a strong no-trump?

1. ♠ A 9 8 5	2. ♠ A K 8	3. ♠ K Q 7 5
♡ K J 7	♡ K 9 7 5	♡ A J 10
◇ Q 9 8	◇ K J 5	◇ K Q 9
♣ K J 7	♣ J 7 4	♣ K 7 4

Answers:

Bids (1 pt. each)   Reasons (1½ pts. each)

1. 1 N.T. if using 'weak'—the right count and no future problems.
   1♣   if using "strong". With both minors qualifying, open 1♣ a 'prepared' bid with insufficient strength for 1 N.T.

2. 1♡   if using 'weak', intending to rebid 1 N.T. to show 15-16 points.
   1 N.T. if using 'strong'—no need to look for any alternative.

3. 1♠   in either case, as the hand is too strong for even a 'strong' no-trump. There's no need to use a 'prepared' minor, so open in your four-card suit.

4A. What opening bids would you make on these 4—4—4—1 hands?

1. ♠ A J 9 8   2. ♠ 7   3. ♠ K J 8 2
   ♡ 7   ♡ 9 8 6 3   ♡ 9 8 6 3
   ◇ K Q 9 3   ◇ A K J 7   ◇ A K J 3
   ♣ A J 10 9   ♣ A Q 10 6   ♣ A

Answers:
Bid (2 pts.)   Reason (3 pts.)

1.   1◇   The basic rule is that with three biddable suits you should open one of the suit below the singleton.

2.   1◇   The hearts can't be considered biddable, so treat the hand as a diamond-club two-suiter, and open one of the higher-ranking of equal and adjacent suits.

3.   1♠   Treat the hand as a spade-diamond two-suiter plus *heart* support. 1♠ is the bid best calculated to facilitate the rest of the auction.

4B. What opening bids would you make on these 4—4—4—1 hands?

1. ♠ A Q 9 8   2. ♠ A Q 9 8   3. ♠ A
   ♡ K 10 7 6   ♡ K Q 9 3   ♡ K 10 7 6
   ◇ 5   ◇ A J 10 9   ◇ A Q 9 8
   ♣ Q 10 5 4   ♣ 7   ♣ Q 10 5 4

Answers:
Bid (2 pts.)   Reason (3 pts.)

1.   No The honour count is not good enough to compensate
      Bid for the lack of playing strength.

2.   1♡   An exception to the rule given in **4A,** No. 1. When the singleton is in clubs, open 1♡ which may facilitate a spade response. Failing this, there is a sensible rebid of 2◇ over 2♣ or a raise if responder bids diamonds.

3.   1♡   The suit below the singleton. Note the difference from No. 1 in this section—the addition of the ♠A makes an opening bid mandatory.

5A. If using a 12-14 pt. no-trump, what opening bids would you make?

	1. ♠ A Q J 7	2. ♠ A Q J 7	3. ♠ A Q J 7
	♡ A K 9 2	♡ J 8 3	♡ 7 4
	◇ J 8 5	◇ A K 9 2	◇ A K 9 2
	♣ 7 4	♣ 7 4	♣ J 8 5

Answers:

Bid (2 pts.)   Reason (3 pts.)

1. 1♠   4-4-3-2 hands which don't qualify for a no-trump opening can be more difficult to bid than 4-4-4-1 hands. Here, however, you simply bid the higher-ranking of equal and adjacent suits.

2. 1♠   Your choice is conditioned by the fact that you have support for hearts. If you open 1◇ and the response is 2♣, you have no sensible rebid.

3. 1◇   The same hand except that now the support is for clubs. 1◇—1♡—1♠ is sensible, but what do you rebid if you open 1♠ and responder bids 2♡?

5B. If using a 12-14 pt. no-trump, what opening bids would you make?

	1. ♠ 7 4	2. ♠ A Q J 7	3. ♠ J 8 3
	♡ A Q J 7	♡ J 8 3	♡ A Q J 7
	◇ J 8 5	◇ 7 4	◇ 7 4
	♣ A K 9 2	♣ A K 9 2	♣ A K 9 2

Answers:

Bid (2 pts.)   Reason (3 pts.)

1. 1♡   This choice is conditioned by the fact that you have support for diamonds. If responder bids 1♠ you can rebid 2♣ or, if he bids 2◇ (probably a five-card suit) raise to 3◇.

2. 1♣   This opening is conditioned by nothing except the fact that, with two black suits of equal length, you should open 1♣.

3. 1♣   If partner responds 1◇ you can rebid 1♡ and if instead he responds 1♠ you are not over-stating your hand if you rebid 1 N.T. Note that none of the six hands on this page is strong enough to show a new suit at the three-level (1♡—2◇—3♣) which is a one-round force.

6A. Using a 12-14 pt. no-trump, what opening bids would you make?

1. ♠ A J 8	2. ♠ A K 8	3. ♠ 9 6 5 2
♡ A Q 6 5 3	♡ A Q 7 5	♡ K Q 6
◇ K 9 8	◇ K J 6 2	◇ A K 8
♣ 7 5	♣ A 8	♣ A J 8

Answers:
Bid (2 pts.)   Reason (3 pts.)

1.   1♡   Although within the limits for a weak no-trump opening, this hand is far better expressed by a 1♡ opening and, if expedient, a heart rebid.

2. 2 N.T.   A perfect hand for this bid, showing 20-22 pts. and an even distribution.

3.   1♠   With 17 pts. this hand is strong enough to open with one of the four-card suit, even if it is a pretty poor one. Don't make the error of falling for a 'prepared' 1♣, a favourite nonsense bid in untutored circles.

6B. Using a 12-14 pt. no-trump, what opening bids would you make?

1. ♠ 10 9 8	2. ♠ A K 8	3. ♠ A Q
♡ A 8 7 5	♡ A Q 7 5	♡ A Q 7
◇ K J 6	◇ K 9 6 2	◇ A Q 9 8 5
♣ A K 3	♣ 9 8	♣ K J 8

Answers:
Bid (2 pts.)   Reason (3 pts.)

1.   1♣   Too good for a weak no-trump, the alternative opening of 1♡ leaves you a difficult rebid if responder bids 2♣ or 2◇. A moment when it is sensible to choose a 'prepared' 1♣.

2.   1♡   Treat the hand as a straightforward red two-suiter, and open one of the higher-ranking of equal and adjacent suits.

3. 2 N.T.   There's no law against opening 2 N.T. with a five-card suit. Besides coming within the prescribed 20-22 pts., this tenace-studded collection is likely to play better with the lead coming up to, rather than through it.

7A. Using a 15-17 pt. no-trump, what opening bids would you
make, and what if you were using a 12-14 pt. no-trump?

1. ♠ A 9 8	2. ♠ A J 9	3. ♠ A Q 9
♡ K J 7 2	♡ K J 7 2	♡ K J 7 2
◇ 9 8 5	◇ Q 8 5	◇ K 9 3
♣ A Q 6	♣ A 7 6	♣ A Q 6

Answers:

Bids (1 pt. each)   Reasons (1½ pts. each)

1. 1♣ Too weak for a 'strong' no-trump so open a 'pre-
        pared' 1♣.

   1 N.T. if using 'weak', and in spite of the diamond weak-
          ness.

2. 1 N.T. 'strong', for which you have the perfect hand.

   1♡ if using 'weak'. No need for a 'prepared' opening
       as with something in every suit you can rebid 2 N.T.
       if responder bids 2♣ or 2◇, and 1 N.T. if he bids 1♠.

3. 1♡ in either case, as the hand is too strong for any variety
        of no-trump. Bid one of the four-card suit and let the
        future take care of itself.

7B. Using a 15-17 no trump, what opening bids would you
make, and what if you were using a 12-14 pt. no-trump?

1. ♠ A 9 8	2. ♠ A J 9 7 2	3. ♠ A Q 9
♡ K J 7 2	♡ K J 2	♡ K J 7 2
◇ A Q 6	◇ Q 8	◇ K 10 8 4
♣ 9 8 5	♣ A 7 6	♣ 6 2

Answers:

Bids (1 pt. each)   Reasons (1½ pts. each)

1. 1◇ Not good enough for a 'strong' no-trump. Bid 1◇,
        not 1♣, as you have no high honour in the latter.

   1 N.T. in spite of the club weakness. It's the most pre-emptive
          of the one-level bids as well as leaving no rebid
          problems.

2. 1♠ in either case as there is nothing against this perfectly
        natural opening which will not cause a rebid problem.

3. 1♡ in both cases. Below the range for a 'strong' no-trump,
        simply treat it as a red two-suiter.

   1 N.T. Use the most pre-emptive one-bid available.

8A. What opening bids would you make on these hands?

1. ♠ A K Q 10 8 5 3	2. ♠ A K J 10 9 6	3. ♠ A J 9 8 5 3 2
♡ K Q 4	♡ A Q J 10 5	♡ K Q 4
◇ 6	◇ K 3	◇ 6
♣ K 3	♣ —	♣ K 3

Answers:
Bid (2 pts.)   Reason (3 pts.)

1.   2♠   Allowing for any reasonable break, this hand contains eight playing tricks at spades–a Strong Two. Do note that you don't count points—count playing tricks.

2.   2♣   Another type of Strong Two, a powerful two-suiter, on which it is vital to ensure a second chance to bid. Here again, don't count points.

3.   1♠   Good as it is, this hand lacks the power required for a Strong Two. Open 1♠ prepared to rebid strongly if partner can make any unforced response.

8B. What opening bids would you make on these hands?

1. ♠ A Q J 9 6 4	2. ♠ 8	3. ♠ A K
♡ 8	♡ A Q J 10 9	♡ A Q J 10 7 5 4
◇ —	◇ A K 10 7 4	◇ 6 2
♣ A K J 8 3 2	♣ 10 5	♣ K 3

Answers:
Bid (2 pts.)   Reason (3 pts.)

1.   2♠   With a hand worth a Strong Two you can't bid 2♣ which would, of course, be conventional. Open 2♠ and make your rebid in clubs. Don't count points.

2.   1♡   Not good enough for more than a one-bid. Open 1♡ and await developments.

3.   2♡   A strong single-suited hand on which you can count a sure eight tricks if played in hearts. Don't count points.

9A. At equal vulnerability, what dealer's opening bid would you make, and would you make the same bid third-in-hand after two passes?

1. ♠ A Q 9 7 6 4 3	2. ♠ 6	3. ♠ K Q J 10 9 6 3 2
♡ 8 5	♡ J 8 5 3	♡ —
◇ 6 2	◇ A Q 9 7 6 4 3	◇ 6 2
♣ J 5	♣ 5	♣ A 9 2

Answers:

Bids (1 pt. each) Reasons (1½ pts. each)

1. 3♠ as dealer. A hand with no defensive values, though 3♠ may interfere with the enemy's bidding sequence.

   3♠ as third-in-hand. Nothing has changed except that fourth-in-hand may be prevented from bidding.

2. No Bid as dealer. Don't warn partner off showing hearts, for which you have excellent support.

   3◇ as third-in-hand after partner's pass. It is now less likely that you have a good heart contract available, and obstruction of the opposition may be given priority.

3. 2♠ as dealer, a normal Strong Two opening bid.

   4♠ as third-in-hand, showing a maximum of two defensive tricks and obstructing any red suit attempt by your opponents.

9B. At equal vulnerability, what dealer's opening bid would you make, and would you make the same bid third-in-hand after two passes?

1. ♠ 7	2. ♠ 6	3. ♠ 8
♡ A Q J 10 8 7 6 3	♡ 7	♡ K J 10 9 7 6 3 2
◇ A 7 2	◇ K 5 4	◇ 7 5 4
♣ 6	♣ A K J 8 6 5 4 3	♣ 6

Answers:

Bids (1 pt. each) Reasons (1½ pts. each)

1. 2♡ as dealer, with eight playing tricks at hearts—a **Strong Two**.

   4♡ as third-in-hand after two passes. You have no hopes of a slam for your side, and obstruction of the opposition is now of great importance.

2. 5♣ as dealer, with a long strong suit and absolutely no defence in either major.

   5♣ as third-in-hand for the same reasons.

3. 3♡ as dealer. No other suit interests you and you want to put a pre-emptive barrier in the path of the enemy.

   3♡ as third-in-hand for the same reasons.

10A. What opening bids would you make?

1. ♠ A K 6 4	2. ♠ A Q J 4	3. ♠ A K 6 4
♡ K 10	♡ A J 6	♡ A 6 4
◇ A K 9 3	◇ K Q 4	◇ A 9 3
♣ A Q 7	♣ A K Q	♣ A 7 2

Answers:
Bid (2 pts.)   Reason (3 pts.)

1. 2♣ This is clearly a no-trump type hand, but as an open-
        ing of 2 N.T. shows 20-22 pts. *only,* here a stronger
        bid is needed. Open 2♣, intending to rebid 2 N.T. to
        show 23-24 pts.

2. 2♣ This hand is even stronger, and too good for 2♣ with
        a 2 N.T. rebid. Open 2♣ intending to rebid 3 N.T.
        to show 25 or more points.

3. 1♠ 19 pts., not strong enough for better than a one-level
        bid, as it has no 'playing strength'. Open 1♠ and
        await developments. You can always force on the next
        round—if any.

10B. What opening bids would you make?

1. ♠ A Q	2. ♠ A 9 8	3. ♠ A J 10
♡ A K 9 2	♡ K Q 9 7	♡ K Q 9 7
◇ A 9 8 7	◇ A K 6	◇ A K 6
♣ K Q 10	♣ K 6 3	♣ A K 3

Answers:
Bid (2 pts.)   Reason (3 pts.)

1. 2 N.T. In addition to showing 20-22 pts., this bid will also tell
           responder how little help you need for a successful
           game contract. Believe it or not, but at a recent duplic-
           ate event, one player chose a 'prepared' 1♣ and had
           only herself to blame when this was passed out. Re-
           sponder had ♠K-x-x and ♣J-9-x-x.

2. 1♡ Just below strength for 2 N.T. Open one of the four-
        card suit, *not* 1♣, which should only be used when
        the hand otherwise lacks a sensible re-bid.

3. 2♣ Too strong for 2 N.T., so open 2♣ intending to rebid
        2 N.T.

11A. What opening bids would you make on these hands?

	1. ♠ K J 6 3	2. ♠ A K Q 7 5	3. ♠ A K Q J 6
	♡ A K J 10 4	♡ A K 9	♡ A 9
	◇ —	◇ 6	◇ A
	♣ A Q 7 2	♣ K Q J 4	♣ K J 9 8 4

Answers:
Bid (2 pts.)   Reason (3 pts.)

1. 1♡ Below strength for better than a one-level bid. Open in your longest suit, prepared to take strong action if partner can bid at all.

2. 2♣ 5 Q.T. as well as immense playing strength. Don't leave partner guessing by making any lesser bid.

3. 2♠ Just below strength for 2♣, which would be conventional, but too good for a one-level bid which might be passed out. A Strong Two opening will ensure a chance to show both suits and hear partner's preference.

11B. What opening bids would you make on these hands?

	1. ♠ A K J 10 6 4	2. ♠ A K J 10 6 4	3. ♠ A K J 10 6 4
	♡ A Q	♡ A 8	♡ A Q
	◇ K Q 9	◇ K 9 8	◇ A K 8
	♣ 7 3	♣ 7 3	♣ 7 3

Answers:
Bid (2 pts.)   Reason (3 pts.)

1. 2♠ Far too good for a one-level opening which might be passed out. Tell partner how little help you need for a successful game contract.

2. 1♠ Short of the values for a stronger opening. You can always bid strongly on the next round if partner can respond.

3. 2♣ All the qualifications for this strongest opening bid. You open 2♣ not just because you like the sound of the bid, but to tell partner how good your hand is. As little as the ◇Q in partner's hand plus a 'lucky' heart lead would give you a game.

12A. What opening bids would you make on these hands?

1. ♠ Q J 10 9 8 7 6 5   2. ♠ A K J 7   3. ♠ A 6
   ♡ —   ♡ 7 3   ♡ A K J 10 7
   ◇ A K   ◇ —   ◇ A J 8
   ♣ A K Q   ♣ A K Q J 10 7 6   ♣ K Q 6

Answers:

Bid (2 pts.)   Reason (3 pts.)

1. 5♠   A conventional opening bid (in the majors only) asking
         partner to bid the Little Slam if he has either the ♠A
         or ♠K, even if singleton. With both he must bid the
         Grand Slam and with neither, however good the rest of
         his hand, he must pass.

2. 2♣   Although slightly under strength, it is permissible to
         open 2♣ when the predominating suit is clubs.

3. 2♣   5+ Q.T. and great playing strength. Tell partner
         this so that he can judge the worth of even a few
         points opposite.

12B. What opening bids would you make on these hands?

1. ♠ —   2. ♣ A 6   3. ♠ K Q J 10 7 5
   ♡ K Q J 10 6   ♡ A Q J 8 7   ♡ 8
   ◇ A   ◇ —   ◇ A K Q
   ♣ A K Q J 10 8 6   ♣ K Q J 10 7 4   ♣ A K Q

Answers:

Bid (2 pts.)   Reason (3 pts.)

1. 4 N.T. Conventional, requesting partner to name his ace or
           aces, if any. If he has the worthless ♠A you will play
           in 6♣, but if he has the ♡A you can bid the Grand
           Slam.

2. 2♡   Although the predominating suit is clubs, it is not
         necessary to devalue a 2♣ opening when there is an
         alternative bid available.

3. 2♣   A Little Slam requires at least one major suit ace from
         partner, failing which you can play quietly in 4♠.
   If the bidding starts 2♣—2◇, you will rebid a conventional 3♠
   to ask if he has any one ace at all.

FIRST ROUND RESPONDING BIDS
The Basic Rules

A RESPONSE in a new suit to a suit opening bid is forcing for one round *unless* the responder has previously passed, a fact which may make a difference to responder's choice of bid. Both no-trump and suit limit bids are available, and these show both the upper and lower limits of the values held, leaving responder under no obligation to bid again unless his partner forces him to do so. In principle, a suit limit bid promises four-card trump support, but there are occasions when this rule has to give way to common sense.

1. *Change of Suit:*

1♡—1♠
or
1◇—1♠ — At the one-level, 6+ pts. with a biddable four-card or longer suit. Forcing for one round unless responder has previously passed. Promises no more strength than 1 N.T. would do.

1♡—2◇
or
1◇—2♣ — At the two-level, a minimum of 8 pts. Stronger responding hand will be shown on the next round.

1♡—3◇
or
1♡—2♠ — A jump of one level more than is necessary is strength-showing and forcing to game. Either a good quality suit or possibly a short suit with good support for opener's suit, or an evenly balanced 16 or more points.

1♡—3♠
or
1◇—4♠ — A jump of two or more levels is pre-emptive, showing weakness except for the suit bid, which will be long.
Used to obstruct the opponents' bidding to the full and also to warn partner of the character of the hand.

1♡—4♣ — 'Swiss' convention, showing 4-card support for partner's major suit opening, two aces, and 13-15 points.
For subsequent development of bidding see p. 104.

1♠—4◇   'Swiss' convention, showing 4-card support for partner's major suit opening, three aces and 13-15 points. Both 4♣ and 4◇ deny the strength for an immediate force.

There are other versions of 'Swiss'.

2. Suit Limit Bids:

1♠—2♠   Weak, showing 6-9 pts. with four-card trump support.

1♡—3♡   Showing four-card trump support, good 'shape', and 10-12 pts. including distribution. Strong and encouraging though not forcing.

1◇—3◇   In the minors, denies ability to bid more constructively, showing at least 10-12 pts., and four-card trump support. Suggests a possible 3 N.T. contract. Again, highly encouraging though not forcing.

3. No-Trump Limit Bids:

1♠—1 N.T.   In response to a major suit opening shows 6-9 pts. in a hand lacking four-card trump support. A weak 'keep open' bid.

1♣—1 N.T.   A more positive bid, showing 8-10 pts., as all other suits are available for a one-level response.

1♡—2 N.T.   In response to any suit opening shows 10-12 pts. in a balanced hand. Encouraging but not forcing.

1♠—3 N.T.   In response to any suit opening shows 13-15 pts. in a balanced hand. Not to be taken as a 'stop' bid. Avoid this response if an alternative is available, as it can hamper possible slam investigations.

4. Responses to Strong Two Openings:

2◇, 2♡,   Strong Two opening bids are unconditionally
2♠   forcing for one round, with a negative response of 2 N.T. on values below one quick trick.

2♡—3♡   Single raise of suit opened shows adequate trump support and at least one ace or void. Unlimited in strength and allowing space for slam investigations.

2♠—4♠ or 2◇—4◇	A double jump to the four level in either major or minor shows adequate trump support, about 10-11 pts. and *no* first-round control (i.e. no ace or void).
2♡—3 N.T.	About 10-12 points, no void, and trump fit too poor for direct raise to the four-level.
2◇—2♡	At least a four-card biddable suit and 8 or more pts., too good for a 2 N.T. negative when the suit can be shown cheaply at the two-level.
2♡—3◇	When the bidding level must be raised, shows at least a five-card biddable suit and 9 or more pts., and denies sufficient support for opener's suit to give a direct raise.
2♡—3♠	A jump take-out in a new suit shows a long, strong and solid suit, at least as good as A-K-Q-J to six or A-K-Q to seven.

5.   Responses to 2♣ Openings:

2♣	The 2♣ opening bid is unconditionally forcing to game unless opener rebids 2 N.T.
2◇	is the first negative response, showing weakness, and less than the values set out below.
2 N.T.	is the second negative if responder is still unable to make any constructive bid after opener's rebid.
2♡, 2♠ 3♣ or 3◇	Positive responses showing a biddable suit (possibly only a four-card suit at the two-level) and a minimum holding of: One ace and one king A biddable suit and 1½ Q.T. Any 8 honour pts.
2 N.T.	Shows any of the above requirements but no biddable suit.

6.   Responses to Pre-emptive Opening Bids:

3♡—4♡	Raise to game on not less than 3-4 honour tricks and some trump fit.
3◇—4♠	Take out into a game contract on strength and own long strong suit.
3♡—3♠	Take-out into a major suit below game level is a one-round force, and opener may raise to game in responder's suit on as little as Q-x in support.

3♡—4♣   Take-out into a minor is also a one-round force and is conveniently used to agree opener's suit as trumps with a possible slam in mind.

3♠—3 N.T.   is to play, inferring fit with opener's suit and/or long suit of own with outside controls.

7. *Responses to Conventional Openings*:

5 of a
major
Pass unless holding either the ace *or* king of the suit opened. Raise to Little Slam with either, even if singleton, and to Grand Slam with both.

6 of a
minor
Pass unless holding either the ace *or* king of the suit opened. Raise to Grand Slam with either, even if singleton.

4 N.T.   With no ace, 5♣: with ♣A, 6♣: with ♢A, ♡A or ♠A, five of the ace-suit: with any two aces, 5 N.T.

FIRST ROUND RESPONDING BIDS

Exercises

♠ ♡ ♣ ◇ ♣ ♡ ♣ ◇ ♠ ♡ ♣ ◇ ♣ ♡ ♣ ◇ ♠ ♡ ♣ ◇ ♠ ♡ ♣ ◇ ♠ ♡ ♣ ◇

No. 1   ♠ K 9 7 2   Your partner deals and opens 1♠.
        ♡ 8 4   What would you respond?
        ◇ Q 9 8 5
        ♣ 10 6 3

Answer : A basic rule for Acol bidding is that if a hand contains the requirements for a limit bid in response to partner's major suit opening, that bid is to be preferred to any other. So on the hand above there is no possible response except 2♠.

A limit bid, though it may be highly encouraging, is never forcing. It tells partner all you have in one simple bid and leaves him to judge whether your combined forces are now worth another try. A single raise, as in this instance, is a very weak response, showing between 6-9 pts., honour plus distributional. One point for the doubleton heart brings this hand up to 6 pts., just worth a raise, if only for the pre-emptive value against fourth-in-hand.

(Bid: 2♠.)

No. 2   ♠ K 9 7   Your partner deals and opens 1♠.
        ♡ J 8 4   What would you respond?
        ◇ Q 9 8 5
        ♣ 10 6 3

Answer : One of the basic requirements for a limit bid in partner's suit is four-card trump support, and though there are occasions when you have to break this rule, this is not one of them. In other words, if there is a sensible alternative, use it.

When partner opens 1♠ this hand is just too good to pass, but you have only three spades and no suit of your own you can bid at the one-level, let alone the two-level. Keep the bidding open with 1 N.T., which again shows 6-9 pts., though this time it *denies* four-card trump support.

(Bid: 1 N.T.)

No. 3   ♠ K 9 5   Your partner deals and opens 1♡.
    ♡ A 9 2   What would you respond?
    ♢ K 9 8 6 4
    ♣ 8 3

Answer : Lacking four-card heart support you look first for a response other than a direct raise in hearts, as it is always unwise to make a misleading bid if a truthful one can be found.

The minimum count required for a change-of-suit response at the two-level is 8 pts., and here you have 10, plus a biddable diamond suit. Bid 2♢ which will tell partner that you are not strong enough to make a game-forcing bid, that you either lack four-card heart support or are too strong to risk an immediate raise to 3♡ which might be passed, and that your hand is not sufficiently evenly-balanced for you to be looking for a no-trump contract at this stage.

(Bid: 2♢.)

No. 4   ♠ Q 9 8   Your partner deals and opens 1♡.
    ♡ 9 7 6 2   What would you respond, and what
    ♢ 7   would you have responded if his
    ♣ A 9 6 4 2   opening bid had been 1♠?

Answer : In the first case you have no problem. In support of a 1♡ opening you have 6 honour pts., 2 distributional pts. (the diamond singleton) and four-card trump support—tailor-made for a limit bid of 2♡.

When the opening bid is 1♠, however, you lack four-card trump support, and nor have you got the 8 pts. you would promise by a change-of-suit to 2♣. Since with 6 pts. you can't possibly pass, you might consider the keep-open bid of 1 N.T. but this, with your singleton diamond, would hardly be realistic. The least of the available evils is to raise 1♠ to 2♠. After all, you have three spades to an honour and a useful 'ruffing value'.

(Bids: 2♡ and 2♠.)

No. 5 ♠ K J 6
      ♡ Q 10 8 5
      ◇ K 10 9 8 5
      ♣ 6

What would you respond to your partner's opening 1♠, and what to his opening 1♡?

Answer : A perfectly natural change-of-suit bid of 2◇ is the correct response to 1♠. Clearly you shouldn't raise spades when you have a sensible alternative, and to bid in no-trumps would be quite unrealistic.

The situation is very different when partner opens 1♡. Now you have excellent four-card trump support as well as the necessary 10-12 pts. (honours + distribution) for a limit bid of 3♡. This, as well as telling partner both the upper and lower limits of your values in one simple bid, is also highly pre-emptive, and may make it impossible for your left-hand opponent to come into the auction at all.

(Bids: 2◇ and 3♡.)

No. 6 ♠ A 10 7 5 4 2
      ♡ 7
      ◇ Q 10 8
      ♣ 7 5 4

What would you respond to your partner's opening 1♡, and what difference would it make if your spade suit were exchanged with your clubs?

Answer : The first question is easily disposed of—you would bid 1♠ which promises no more than a bid of 1 N.T. would do, except that it shows a biddable spade suit.

Mentally exchanging your two black suits, you can't support hearts so your choice, since you can't consider passing, is between 1 N.T., for which you have the right count but not the 'shape', and 2♣, for which you have the shape but not the count! The choice that distorts the picture of your hand the least is 2♣.

Acol players aim to tell the truth when they make a bid, but if this is absolutely impossible, they try to tell the whitest lie available.

(Bids: 1♠ and 2♣.)

No. 7   ♠ A Q 8   Your partner deals and opens 1◇.
      ♡ 9 3 2   What would you respond?
      ◇ J 9 7 6
      ♣ 10 9 8

Answer : The limit bids, that is, the direct raises in partner's bid
suit, are just as much available in the minors as in the majors. But
there is this difference—five of a minor for a game is a long way
to go when 3 N.T. may be an easier contract. The actual values
required for a direct minor suit raise to either the two or the
three-level are the same as for the major suits but, particularly
when you have not previously passed, you should make sure there
is no possibly more constructive bid you can make.

On this hand there is nothing you can honestly do except raise
1◇ to 2◇. Your only possible alternative is 1 N.T., but your
partner will have at least three diamonds to a high honour, and
probably more. To know that you have four diamonds in a weak
hand won't deter him from bidding on if he himself is strong.

(Bid: 2◇.)

No. 8   ♠ A 10 8 6   Your partner deals and opens 1◇.
      ♡ K 8 7 2   What would you respond, and would
      ◇ J 10 8   it make any difference if your ♣9
      ♣ 9 3   were the ♣A?

Answer: Holding two four-card suits in a weak hand worth only
one forward-going move, it is better to respond in the lower-
ranking first, which is best calculated to facilitate the rest of the
auction. An exception to this is when the lower-ranking suit is too
weak to suggest as trumps which would be the case if, for instance,
your ♡ K and ♣9 were exchanged for the ♡ 9 and ♣ K. The
correct response as the hand is, is 1♡.

If you added the ♣ A, four more honour points, the hand
becomes worth at least a second forward move, but the best
response would still be 1♡.

(Bids: 1♡ and 1♡.)

No. 9 ♠ A Q 8
♥ Q 9 8 6
♦ J 9 8 7
♣ 6 3

Your partner deals and opens 1♦. What would you respond, and would it make any difference if you had dealt and passed originally?

Answer : When you have not previously passed you should make what may possibly be a constructive bid of 1♡. This is, after all, a one-round force, so if it doesn't help partner into a no-trump contract, there will always be time to put him back into diamonds.

If you had dealt and passed originally, your change of suit to 1♡ would no longer be forcing and partner, with a reasonable three-card heart fit, might well pass when the hand belongs in diamonds. It, therefore, becomes far wiser to settle for a limit bid of 3♦ because of the risk that you may never get a chance to put partner back to this suit.

(Bids : 1♡ and 3♦.)

No. 10 ♣ Q 8 7
♥ Q 9 8
♦ J 9 8 7
♣ J 8 3

Your partner deals and opens 1♣. What would you respond? Would it make any difference if your spades were ♠A-Q-8 instead of ♠Q-8-7?

Answer : With the hand as it is you should respond 1♦ to partner's 1♣ because—and this is the important point—you are not strong enough to respond 1 N.T. to a 1♣ opening.

With the other three suits all available for a one-level response, or even perhaps a raise of 1♣ to 2♣ if that is your only four-card suit, Acol players keep a response of 1 N.T. to 1♣ as a positive bid showing 8-10 pts., not the mere 6-9 pts. it would show in response to any other suit.

With the spades topped up by the ♠A you could, it is true, still respond 1♦, but it is a far more constructive bid to show that your count, without any good biddable suit, is 8-10 pts., so in this second situation 1 N.T. would be the best response.

(Bids: 1♦ and 1 N.T.)

No. 11 ♠ K J 6
      ♥ J 9 5
      ♦ Q 9 8 5
      ♣ A 8 5

Your partner deals and opens 1♠. What would you respond, and would it make any difference if you had dealt and passed originally?

Answer : Limit bids in the major suits or in no-trumps are not affected in any way by your position at the table though they can, of course, be affected by intervening bids. Here there is no intervention to contend with. Not strong enough to open, though with one more point you could have opened a 12-14 pt. no-trump if no one had spoken before you, you have, whether you've already had the chance to pass or not, a perfect limited response of 2 N.T.

Your only possible alternative is a change of suit response of 2♦, but 2 N.T. will tell partner in the one single bid that you have an evenly balanced hand of 10-12 pts, and no five-card suit.

                      (Bids: 2 N.T. in either case.)

No. 12 ♠ K J 6
      ♥ J 9 5
      ♦ Q 9 8 5
      ♣ A Q 5

Your partner deals and opens 1♥. What would you respond?

Answer : You will note that you are not asked what you would respond if you had previously passed because you would, of course, have opened on this hand, either 1 N.T. or 1♣ according to the strength of the no-trump being used.

Just occasionally hands crop up on which the only sensible response is an immediate 3 N.T. This shows 13-15 pts. and obviously partner, with a strong opening hand, must take it as encouragement to go on rather than as a 'stop' bid. However, bidding on can be difficult at the high level reached, for which reason it is a response to be avoided if a more constructive one can be found. Here there is no more constructive alternative available and it is, in fact, a typical hand for the bid.

                              (Bid: 3 N.T.)

No. 13 ♠ J 9 7 5 4   At Game to your opponents your
       ♡ 8 3   partner deals and opens 1♠. Your
       ◇ 9   right hand opponent passes—what
       ♣ K Q 10 8 5   would you bid?

Answer: An intervening bid on your right hand would, in fact, make no difference. The best thing you can do, particularly at the score, is to jump direct to 4♠. This is a highly pre-emptive measure, designed to make life as difficult as possible for your left hand opponent who, if he wants to bid, will now be forced to start his operations at a very high level. He may, in consequence, be quite unable to discover his own best spot—or even if he has one!

In the early days of the Acol System, this direct jump to the four-level was used as a limit bid, even stronger than a bid at the three-level. Nowadays, however, there is other machinery available for the strong hands, and the four-level bid is purely pre-emptive. Trump fit and distribution are the clues.

(Bid: 4♠.)

No. 14 ♠ 9   At Game to your opponents your
       ♡ 6 5   partner deals and opens 1◇. Your
       ◇ K Q 10 8 6 right hand opponent passes—what
       ♣ Q J 10 8 3   would you bid?

Answer : Trump support, 'shape', and above all, no defence whatsoever in the majors, make this hand suitable for a highly pre-emptive jump to 4◇. As in No. 13, note the useful club side suit.

Weakness, particularly in the majors, is an essential for this bid which, of course, precludes any chance of your side playing in 3 N.T. So if partner wants to go on to game, it will have to be in diamonds, though he is at liberty to pass the four-level bid if he thinks fit. Whichever he chooses, he will know that he is facing weakness, though that he can at least be sure of trump length in your hand.

(Bid: 4◇.)

No. 15 ♠ 9 6   Your partner deals and opens 1♡.
        ♡ K 9 8 5   What would you respond?
        ◇ A Q 9 2
        ♣ K J 10

Answer : Thinking back to No. 5 in this section, you may have
considered a 3♡ limit bid, but this shows, in addition to the
minimum of four-card trump support, a count of 10-12 pts., *no
more.* Furthermore, a limit bid, even at this encouragingly high
level, is not forcing. Partner could pass and, facing your powerful
hand, a game might well be missed, let alone a slam if he happens
to be strong for his bid.

The answer is to use a Delayed Game Raise, that is, a change
of suit bid as your immediate response, and then a jump bid to
game level on the next round, whether partner merely rebids his
hearts or not. This will show him that you were too strong for
a limit bid whilst, of course, not quite strong enough for a forcing
take-out.

(Bid: 2◇.)

No. 16 ♠ 9 6   Your partner deals and opens 1♡.
        ♡ A 9 8 5   What would you respond?
        ◇ A Q 9 2
        ♣ A 10 9

Answer : This hand differs from No. 15 in that the four points
in clubs are the ace instead of the K-J, yet this makes all the
difference to the best response.

The 'Swiss' Convention, which allows the pin-pointing of controls as well as giving the assurance of four-card trump support,
is the answer this time. There are various versions of this convention, so it's as well to be sure that you and your partner are using
the same one. But the one advocated in *All About Acol* uses an
immediate response of 4♣ to partner's major suit opening bid
to show two aces, four-card trump support, and 13-15 points. 4 ◇
shows the same trump support and three aces, again with 13-15
points. We shall see how the bidding develops after that in
later sections but, meanwhile, respond 4◇ on this hand, not
because you have a diamond suit, but because you have a specific
holding whilst wanting to insist on at least a game contract.

(Bid: 4◇.)

No. 17 ♠ Q 9 6   Your partner deals and opens 1♠.
      ♡ K 6   What would you respond?
      ◇ A Q 7
      ♣ A Q 9 7 5

Answer: You are far too strong for anything other than an immediate game force of 3♣. The ♠Q-x-x is anything but a misfit and in any case, whatever the final denomination, you already know that the hand must be played in at least a game, if not a slam.

When making a forcing take-out choose, if possible, a suit in which you have first-round control and also, provided you are willing to play in partner's bid suit, one which ranks below his. This is not always possible, but bear these two principles in mind. Also, and this is equally important, once you have made your force, don't insist on bidding on to a slam unless you have extra concealed strength in your hand. After all, you will already have said 'game certain, slam possible', a hint which partner should be able to take unless his hand is near minimum.

(Bid; 3♣.)

No. 18 ♠ Q 9 6 4   Your partner deals and opens 1♠.
      ♡ A 7 3   What would you respond, and would
      ◇ A Q 10 8 2 it make any difference if your ♡7
      ♣ 7   became the ♡K?

Answer: As the hand is now it contains a perfect 4♣ 'Swiss' bid, four-card spade support, two aces, and 13-15 points.

Add the ♡K, and it would be too strong for a 'Swiss' response, even though it would still contain the specific holdings promised by the 4♣ bid. The correct response would be 3◇.

You will see that each response has its alloted place, not taking the place of any other. The limit bids either in no-trumps or the suit opened show certain strength whilst denying anything more, the 'Swiss' bids show specific holdings and demand at least a game contract whilst denying the strength to force, and so on.

(Bids: 4♣ and 3◇.)

No. 19   ♠ K 9 8 4   Your partner deals and opens 2♠,
        ♡ A Q 10 7 3   an Acol Strong Two. What would
        ◊ 9 3   you respond?
        ♣ 9 7

Answer : When partner opens with a Strong Two and you are
in agreement with him that this will make a good trump suit, in
other words, when you have a trump fit, immediate support is by
far the most likely response to help him. Obviously, it doesn't
really matter if he has one long suit or is two-suited—you are
with him in the first bid suit. Tell him so by the appropriate raise,
in this case a single raise to 3♠ which, in addition to promising
good (not necessarily four-card) trump support, also shows 'positive' values and at least one ace or void.

Opener, with this much knowledge, can now settle for a mere
game contract or take further steps towards investigating a possible
slam. So here support spades, and don't show the hearts first.

(Bid : 3♠.)

No. 20   ♠ K 9 8 4   Your partner deals and opens 2♠,
        ♡ K Q J 7 3   an Acol Strong Two. What would
        ◊ 9 3   you respond?
        ♣ 9 7

Answer : This hand has exactly the same number of points and
the same excellent spade support as in No. 19, but there is one
important difference, and that is that it has no first-round controls,
either aces or voids, even though it has the values for a 'positive'
response.

You can tell partner all this by bidding an immediate 4♠ from
which he will know that, if he has any ideas of bidding a slam, he
will have to provide at least three first-round controls himself.

Note the difference—a single raise is unlimited, merely agreeing
trumps and promising at least one ace or void. A double raise
also promises trump support but denies an ace or void.

(Bid : 4♠.)

No. 21 ♠ K 10 8 6 5   Your partner deals and opens 2♡,
       ♡ 10 8 5 2   an Acol Strong Two. What would
       ◇ J 6   you respond?
       ♣ 9 6

Answer: You must, at this stage, deny the values for a 'positive' response by giving the negative answer of 2 N.T. If you raise 2♡ to 3♡ you would be promising at least one ace or void and if you raise direct to 4♡, as in No. 20, you would promise at least a trick somewhere, even if it were not an ace or void. After all, your partner won't pass your 2 N.T., so even if he turns out to be two-suited, not single-suited in hearts, you will have a chance to put him back to hearts, for which you have excellent support. In fact you would certainly put him to 4♡ if he merely rebid 3♡ over your 2 N.T. Part of the reason for opening a Strong Two is to tell partner what a good hand you have, and how little help you need to make a game.

(Bid: 2 N.T.)

No. 22 ♠ K 10 9 2   Your partner deals and opens 2◇,
       ♡ Q J 3   an Acol Strong Two. What would
       ◇ 9 8   you respond, and would it make
       ♣ K J 10 7   any difference if he had opened 2♡
                        or 2♠ instead?

Answer: When partner bids 2◇ you can't do that most helpful thing, agree trumps, and nor have you a suit really good enough to wish to suggest as an alternative. You are also much too good to give a 'negative' response, and the correct bid is 3 N.T., which is the approximate equivalent of a 2 N.T. limit bid facing a one-level opening except that, in this case, it denies an ace or void.

If partner had opened 2♡ or 3♣ you would raise direct to four in either suit. You don't need four-card support for a suit good enough to be opened at the two-level, and though you have this in spades, ♡Q-J-x is more than adequate (Q-x-x would be amply good enough) in hearts.

(Bids: 3 N.T., 4♡, and 4♣.)

No. 23 ♠ K 9 8 3
      ♥ J 10 8
      ♦ 8 7 6
      ♣ 10 4 3

Your partner deals and opens 1♥. What would you respond and what difference would it make if he had opened 2♥?

Answer : With only four points and no 'shape' whatsoever, there's only one thing you can sensibly do when partner opens at the one-level, and that's say No Bid. Even had he opened 1♣, for which you have at least a four-card fit, the lower the contract the better from your point of view.

When partner opens 2♥ you have no option. This bid is forcing for one round, so you would have to bid the 'negative' 2 N.T.

If anyone ever tells you it is stupid to keep a Strong Two open even for one round on a near Yarborough, remember that partner may have game 'cold' in his own hand and, if he can't rely on you to let him have his chance to bid it, he will be forced into devaluing his 2♣ openings on any occasion when a second chance to bid is essential to him.

(Bids: No Bid and 2 N.T.)

No. 24 ♠ K 9 7 2
      ♥ Q 5 4
      ♦ 9
      ♣ 10 9 8 5 4

Your partner deals and opens 2♣. What would you respond?

Answer : This conventional opening bid is the announcement of an extremely powerful hand, though at this stage you don't know whether it is of no-trump type or based on one or more good suits. For the moment this is not your concern—you will learn more when you have heard your partner's rebid.

In the meantime your correct response is 2♦, for no other reason than that you have such a poor hand that you can only make a negative response.

When it comes to making a positive response you will find a good deal of common sense applies, as it will when a possible rebid is in question. For the moment, however, just keep the bidding open and await developments.

(Bid: 2♦.)

No. 25 ♠ Q 8 5   Your partner deals and opens 2♣.
        ♡ K Q 10 7 5   What would you respond and would
        ◇ J 5   it make any difference if your red
        ♣ 10 4 2   suits were exchanged?

Answer : With the hand as it is when partner opens 2♣ your biddable heart suit, headed by a full quick trick and with the outside value of the ♠Q makes it worth a 'positive' response of 2♡. This, as you can see, doesn't promise a very great deal, and opener won't get over-enthusiastic or expect that a slam must be available.

Exchanging the two red suits would mean that, in order to give a positive response showing diamonds, you would have to bid 3◇ because, as you will remember, 2◇ is the negative. You really are not good enough to raise the bidding to this level, so it would be wiser to bid the negative 2◇ in the first place, and then to take any opportunity of encouraging, to show that, even if negative, your hand is not worthless.

(Bids: 2♡ and 2◇.)

No. 26 ♠ Q 9 7   Your partner deals and opens 2♣.
        ♡ K 9 8   What would you respond and would
        ◇ Q J 6   it make any difference if your black
        ♣ K J 8 7   suits were exchanged?

Answer : With the hand as it is, containing 12 pts. and no really 'biddable' suit, you are much too good for a negative response of 2◇. You could, of course, make a positive response of 3♣, but this uses a good deal of bidding space simply for the sake of mentioning a suit in which you are not really anxious to play. Bid a positive 2 N.T., and await developments.

A four-card major suit is always 'biddable' so, if your clubs and spades were exchanged, it would be more economical in bidding space to make your positive response 2♠ rather than 2 N.T. In other words, if you can show a biddable suit without raising the level of the bidding, do so, but bear in mind that, in practice, it is wiser to conceal even a four-card major unless it is headed by at least the K-J.

(Bids: 2 N.T. and 2♠.)

No. 27 ♠ K J 9
       ♡ A K Q 10
       ◇ A Q J 9 6
       ♣ 9

Your partner deals and opens with a pre-emptive 3♠. What, if anything, would you respond?

Answer: Unfortunately sometimes, when partner has a hand on which he wants to make a pre-emptive bid, it is responder who is in trouble, when he himself has a very powerful hand. However, there are guiding principles to help.

Just as a change-of-suit at the one-level is a one round force, so a change-of-suit at this high level is also a one round force, provided it is a bid below game level. In principle a major suit bid, if not already at game level (as 3♡-3♠), is a game try, and a minor suit bid is a slam try agreeing opener's suit as trumps.

In this case, therefore, responder should bid 4◇, not because he wants to play in this suit but because he is perfectly willing to play in spades. Opener should now show any other feature his hand may contain, but the least he will do is rebid his suit.

(Bid: 4◇.)

No. 28 ♠ 8 2
       ♡ K J 10 9 5 4 3
       ◇ 7 2
       ♣ A K

Your partner deals and opens with a pre-emptive 3♠. What would you respond?

Answer: The most elementary rule for responding to partner's pre-emptive opening is never to rescue into a suit which you have absolutely no guarantee will make a safer contract than his. There's just one thing to do here, and that's to pass—partner's spades may even be better than your hearts, and in addition to side-suit values, you have a doubleton spade for him.

Exchange your major suits, giving yourself long spades and let partner open 3♡, and you would still pass. Remember that 3♠ would be a one-round force, so the contract would have to climb to the four-level. If you had a long and solid suit in addition to your ♣A-K, it would be only sensible to bid it at game level, which your partner could hardly misunderstand.

(Bid: No Bid.)

No. 29 ♠ 9 3   Your partner deals and opens 5♠.
      ♡ 4 3   What would you respond?
      ◇ A K 6
      ♣ A K J 9 6 4

Answer : By using this conventional opening bid, your partner is saying that nothing is any use to him except either the ace or king of his trump suit. If he has made the correct opening bid, which you must, of course, assume, you can expect him to have very long spades headed by the ♠Q-J-10, top hearts, and voids in both minors, so your diamond and club honours will be useless.

With either the ace or king of spades, even if singleton, you would raise to 6♠ and with both you would raise to 7♠. With neither you pass, which is only answering the question you have been asked.   (Bid : No Bid.)

No. 30 ♠ K Q J 9 7 4   Your partner deals and opens 4
      ♡ A 7 4 3   N.T. What would you respond?
      ◇ 9 6
      ♣ 8

Answer : 4 N.T. is another conventional opening bid which requires *only* the answer to the question you have been asked— have you any ace at all, and if so, which? Doubtless opener has a hand on which he fears that if he finally enquires about your ace-holding via a 'Blackwood' 4 N.T., he may find it difficult to know whether a 5◇ one-ace response shows the ace he vitally needs or a worthless one.

In response to a 4 N.T. opening you must ignore anything in your hand other than aces. With no ace bid 5♣. With one ace, cue-bid it, that is, with the ◇A, ♡A, or ♠A, bid five of that suit or, with the ♣A, bid 6♣. With two aces, bid 5 N.T. So here you cue-bid your ♡A.

          (Bid : 5♡.)

FIRST ROUND RESPONDING BIDS
Competition Quiz

♠♡♣♢ ♠♡♣♢ ♠♡♣♢ ♠♡♣♢ ♠♡♣♢ ♠♡♣♢ ♠♡♣♢

IN competition against another player, one should answer the three questions in the **A** set, and the other the three questions in the **B** set on each page.

1A. Your partner deals and opens 1♡. What would you respond?

1. ♠ A J 9 4	2. ♠ 9	3. ♠ J 8 6
♡ J 8 6	♡ Q 8 6	♡ A J 9 4
♢ 7 5 4	♢ A 9 7 6 4	♢ J 10 2
♣ J 10 2	♣ 9 8 6 5	♣ 7 5 4

Answers:

Bid (2 pts.)   Reason (3 pts.)

1.   1♠   This change-of-suit promises no more than 1 N.T. would do.

2.   2♡   A single raise of partner's suit normally promises four-card trump support, but 2♡ is more realistic than 1 N.T. or 2♢.

3.   2♡   This is a genuine limit bid, between 6-9 pts. and four-card trump support.

1B. Your partner deals and opens 1♡. What would you respond?

1. ♠ Q 9 5	2. ♠ Q 9	3. ♠ Q 9 5
♡ Q 9 7	♡ J 9 7 2	♡ Q 9 7
♢ K Q 8 7 4	♢ K Q 8 7 4	♢ J 10 8 7 4
♣ Q 8	♣ 9 8	♣ Q 8

Answers:

Bid (2 pts.)   Reason (3 pts.)

1.   2♢   Lacking four-card heart support, you have the necessary minimum of 8 pts. for a change-of-suit response at the two-level.

2.   2♡   A normal limit bid on 6-9 pts. and four-card trump support. Don't 'change the suit' to 2♢ when you needn't.

3. 1 N.T.   You lack four-card trump support but, with at least a doubleton honour in each suit, there is no need to "bend" the rule by raising hearts. Bid 1 N.T.

2A. Your partner deals and opens 1♣. What would you respond?

1. ♠ 9 8 6 3	2. ♠ 9 8 6	3. ♠ 9 8 6
♡ K 7 4	♡ K 7 4	♡ K J 4 3
◇ Q J 5	◇ Q J 5	◇ Q J 5
♣ J 9 7	♣ Q J 9 7	♣ Q J 7

Answers:
Bid (2 pts.)   Reason (3 pts.)

1. 1♠   Your hand is not strong enough for a response of 1 N.T., which shows 8-10 pts. when facing a 1♣ opening. 1♠ at this stage only confirms that you have a little something.

2. 1 N.T.   This count-showing response is likely to be far more constructive than a raise in clubs. Opener will know you have between 8-10 points and, automatically, some fit for clubs.

3.   1♡   Even though you have 10 points on which you could respond 1 N.T., you have a biddable heart suit which might be useful. As the bid is a one-round force you are sure of a chance to bid again if it seems expedient.

2B. Your partner deals and opens 1◇. What would you respond?

1. ♠ J 8 6 3	2. ♠ 9 8 6	3. ♠ 9 8 6
♡ K 7 4	♡ K 7 4	♡ K 7 4
◇ Q J 5	◇ Q J 5 3	◇ Q J 5
♣ J 10 7	♣ J 10 7	♣ J 10 7 3

Answers:
Bid (2 pts.)   Reason (3 pts.)

1.   1♠   You have, in fact, a choice between 1♠ and 1 N.T., but 1♠ is the better.

2.   2◇   Again you have a choice, 1 N.T. or 2◇, but the latter is the better, as you have at least got four-card diamond support, and no stop in spades this time.

3. 1 N.T.   Even without any stop in spades your only sensible bid is 1 N.T., which shows your 6-9 pts, as well as keeping the bidding open in case partner is strong.

3A. Your partner deals and opens 1♠. What would you respond?

1. ♠ Q 10 9   2. ♠ Q 9 7 2   3. ♠ 8 6 5 4
   ♡ Q J 4   ♡ Q J 7   ♡ K 6
   ◇ A 9 7 2   ◇ A 9 7   ◇ A K 9 5 4
   ♣ Q 10 6   ♣ Q 10 6   ♣ 6 3

Answers:
Bid (2 pts.)   Reason (3 pts.)

1. 2 N.T. This is another of the Acol Limit Bids and though not
           forcing, is encouraging. It shows 10-12 pts. on an
           evenly-balanced hand, and denies four-card support for
           partner's major suit opening.

2.   3♠   Here you have four-card spade support and the neces-
           sary 10-12 pts. A non-forcing but encouraging Limit
           Bid, raising the auction to a dangerously high level
           if your left-hand opponent wants to come in.

3.   3♠   This limit bid, guaranteeing four-card trump support,
           is far better Acol technique than a change-of-suit to
           2◇. Announce your full strength in one bid, promising
           10-12 points and 4-card trumps support. *Don't* be
           tempted to bid your diamonds.

3B. Your partner deals and opens 1◇. What would you respond?

1. ♠ 9 8 7 5   2. ♠ A 7 2   3. ♠ Q 7
   ♡ A Q J 6 2   ♡ 10 6 5   ♡ 10 9 6
   ◇ K 3   ◇ K J 6 2   ◇ Q 8 4
   ♣ 9 3   ♣ K 9 2   ♣ A Q J 6 2

Answers:
Bid (2 pts.)   Reason (3 pts.)

1.   1♡   A perfectly normal change-of-suit response showing a
           biddable suit. You choose your longest suit, hearts.

2.   3◇   With the values for a limit bid at the three-level and
           no more constructive bid available, this is your best
           choice. If partner takes out into 3 N.T., which your
           strong raise invites, pass happily.

3.   2♣   Quite unsuitable for a bid in no-trumps at this stage and
           also not fitted for a diamond raise. You have the
           strength for a change-of-suit at the two-level.

4A. Your partner deals and opens 1♡. What would you respond and would it make any difference if you had dealt and passed originally?

1. ♠ 9 3	2. ♠ 9 7 5	3. ♠ 8 5 3
♡ J 9 8 6 2	♡ 10 9	♡ K 9 7 2
◇ 6	◇ A Q J 6 4	◇ 4
♣ K Q J 6 4	♣ K 6 5	♣ K Q J 8 2

Answers:

Bids (1 pt. each)   Reasons (1½ pts. each)

1.   4♡   A pre-emptive attempt to keep your left-hand opponent out of the auction.

      3♡   As you know your left hand opponent could not open, he is hardly likely to be able to come in over 3♡.

2.   2◇   A simple change-of-suit response for which you have the values.

      2◇   Exactly the same—you only just failed to open!

3.   3♡   Full values for the straight limit bid. Position at the
      3♡   table or interference by your opponents makes no difference.

4B. Your partner deals and opens 1◇. What would you respond and would it make any difference if you had dealt and passed originally?

1. ♠ J 10 4	2. ♠ J 10 4	3. ♠ K 9 2
♡ A 10 7	♡ A 10 7 4	♡ Q 7 4
◇ J 8 7 6	◇ J 8 7 6	◇ J 8 7 6
♣ 6 3 2	♣ 6 2	♣ A Q 6

Answers:

Bids (1 pt. each)   Reasons (1½ pts. each)

1.   2◇   This is the only sensible response in either situation.

      2◇   The fact that you have already passed makes no difference.

2.   1♡   This may prove to be the most constructive response and you will always have a chance to put opener back into diamonds.

      2◇   Once having passed, 1♡ would not be forcing, and there is a risk of being left in this contract when the hand 'belongs' in diamonds.

3. 2 N.T.   The 10-12 pt. limit bid in either case. Your only alter-
   2 N.T.   native is 3◇, but it is more likely to encourage partner into a 3 N.T. contract to show your evenly-balanced shape rather than raise diamonds.

5A. Your partner deals and opens 1♡. What would you respond?

1. ♠ 8	2. ♠ A K Q J 9 5 4	3. ♠ K Q 10 6 4
♡ K Q 10 6	♡ 7	♡ 8
◇ K Q 9 4 3	◇ A 6	◇ K Q 9 3
♣ A K 7	♣ 6 3 2	♣ A K 7

Answers:

Bid (2 pts.)   Reason (3 pts.)

1.   3♣   Knowing that the hand will play eventually in hearts, make a forcing bid of 3♣ (choosing the suit in which you have the best 'tops'). This announces 'game certain, slam possible'.

2.   2♠   If you don't make a forcing bid immediately you may find yourself in difficulties on the next round.

3.   1♠   The same honour count as No. 1 but with the complete lack of fit for partner's bid suit it is better to make a simple one-round force and await developments. You can always make a forcing rebid.

5B. Your partner deals and opens 1♡. What would you respond?

1. ♠ A Q J 9 3	2. ♠ K J 2	3. ♠ K Q 5
♡ K J 6	♡ 6	♡ Q 3
◇ K J 5 2	◇ A K 10 9 5	◇ A K J 9 5
♣ 9	♣ K Q 7 4	♣ J 10 7

Answers:

Bid (2 pts.)   Reason (3 pts.)

1.   2♠   Another hand where an immediate force is mandatory. The heart fit is excellent, a game is as near certain as anything could be, and a slam is quite probable, particularly if opener has diamond tops for you.

2.   2◇   The complete lack of a heart fit makes it wiser to go slowly here. You can always force on the next round if expedient.

3.   3◇   The ♡Q-x is by no means a misfit and the force, after all, only commits you to a game, not necessarily to an astronomical contract.

6A. Your partner deals and opens 1♡. What would you respond?

1. ♠ K J 6	2. ♠ A J 7	3. ♠ K 9 6
♡ K 10 7 6	♡ K J 7 6	♡ K 10 8 3
◇ A Q J 8	◇ A Q J 8	◇ A J 9 8
♣ 9 3	♣ J 10	♣ 9 3

Answers:

Bid (2 pts.)   Reason (3 pts.)

1.   2◇   This hand is too strong for a limit bid of 3♡ which might be passed, and it's not quite strong enough for a forcing response. The way to deal with it is via a Delayed Game Raise, 2◇ on the first round and a jump to game next.

2.   3◇   Too strong for either a limit bid or the Delayed Game Raise technique. Make an immediate game force, choosing the suit ranking below the bid suit in which you have 'tops'.

3.   3♡   A straightforward limit bif showing 10-12 pts. and four-card heart support.

6B. Your partner deals and opens 1♣. What would you respond?

1. ♠ J 10 8 7	2. ♠ K J 6 2	3. ♠ K J 6 2
♡ —	♡ J 7 4	♡ J 7 4
◇ A K J 9	◇ A J 7 2	◇ 8 5
♣ K Q 10 7 4	♣ 8 5	♣ A K Q 6

Answers:

Bid (2 pts.)   Reason (3 pts.)

1.   3◇   Too strong for anything other than an immediate force. Note that you choose the suit in which you have the A-K rather than the longer clubs. You are fully prepared to play in spades and you will find that partner will expect first round control of the suit in which you force.

2.   3♠   The straightforward limit bid again, with ten honour points and one distributional point (the doubleton club).

3.   2♣   Too strong for a limit bid and not quite strong enough to force. Respond 2♣ intending to raise to 4♠ if opener rebids 2◇, 2♡, or 2♠.

7A. Your partner deals and opens 1♡. What would you respond?

1. ♠ A 9 3 2	2. ♠ A 9 3 2	3. ♠ A 9 3
♡ K Q 8 4	♡ K 9 8 4	♡ A J 8 4
◇ A 10 6 4	◇ K J 10 6	◇ A 10 6 4
♣ 3 2	♣ 3	♣ 3 2

Answers:

Bid (2 pts.)   Reason (3 pts.)

1.   4♣   This is a 'Swiss' conventional response. There are several versions of this convention but one excellent one uses a response of 4♣ to show four-card trump support, two aces, and 13-15 points. The hand is too good for a limit bid of 3♡ and not good enough for an immediate force.

2.   1♠   The same count as No. 1 but lacking the specific requirement of two aces. Too strong for a 3♡ limit bid, so use the Delayed Game Raise technique.

3.   4◇   A 'Swiss' conventional bid, again showing four-card trump support and three aces in a 13-15 point hand.

7B. Your partner deals and opens 1♠. What would you respond?

1. ♠ K J 8 3	2. ♠ K J 8	3. ♠ A 9 3 2
♡ A 10 6 4	♡ A 10 6	♡ A 10 7 4
◇ 8	◇ A J 8 3 2	◇ 8
♣ J 10 9 3	♣ 3 2	♣ K J 6 2

Answers:

Bid (2 pts.)   Reason (3 pts.)

1.   3♠   Counting 2 pts. for the singleton diamond, this is a perfect hand for this strong limit bid.

2.   2◇   Although you have two aces and good trump support, you can't make a spade limit bid or a 'Swiss' bid at this stage. If partner *re*bids spades over your 2◇, you can put him to 4♠, as then you will know he has at least a five-card suit.

3.   4♣   The 'Swiss' response showing four-card trump support, two aces, and 13-15 points with insufficient strength to make a forcing take-out, though being unwilling to play below game-level.

8A. Your partner deals and opens 1♠. What would you respond?

1. ♠ K 10 8 4	2. ♠ K 10 8 4	3. ♠ K 10 8 4
♡ K 9 3	♡ A 9 3	♡ A 9 3
◇ Q 4	◇ Q 4	◇ A Q
♣ 9 8 4 2	♣ K Q 9 8	♣ 9 8 4 2

Answers:

Bid (2 pts.)   Reason (3 pts.)

1.   2♠   The simple limit bid confirming four-card trump support and the inability to make any stronger bid.

2.   2♣   Too strong for a limit bid which might be passed out, not strong enough for a force, and an immediate 4♠ might cost a missed slam. A Delayed Game Raise starting with a 2♣ change-of-suit is indicated.

3.   4♣   The 'Swiss' bid showing the trump fit, two aces, and 13-15 points.

8B. Your partner deals and opens 1♠. What would you respond?

1. ♠ K Q 8 4	2. ♠ J 10 8 7 6	3. ♠ K 10 8 4
♡ A 9 3	♡ 5 4	♡ A 9 3
◇ A K	◇ K Q J 6 2	◇ Q J
♣ 9 8 4 2	♣ 5	♣ 9 8 4 2

Answers:

Bid (2 pts.)   Reason (3 pts.)

1.   3◇   Much too strong for anything but an immediate game force proclaiming 'game certain, slam possible'.

2.   4♠   This is not a limit bid intended to encourage partner to explore for a slam. It says that you think there should be a play for game on your 'shape' and that you want to try to pre-empt your left-hand opponent out of the auction.

3.   3♠   A straightforward encouraging limit bid showing four-card trump support and 10-12 high card and distributional points.

9A. Your partner deals and opens 2♡. What would you respond?

	1. ♠ K 9 8 4 2	2. ♠ K 9 8 4 2	3. ♠ Q 9 8 4 2
	♡ 7 6	♡ A 7 2	♡ K 7 2
	◇ A 9 3	◇ 7 6 4	◇ 7 6 4
	♣ 8 4 2	♣ 9 7	♣ 8 4 2

Answers:
Bid (2 pts.)   Reason (3 pts.)

1. 2♠   Just worth a 'positive' response as this can be given without raising the level of the auction.

2. 3♡   Any positive response to a Strong Two makes the sequence forcing to game, but it is better to confirm partner's suit as trumps at once, far more likely to interest him than 2♠.

3. 2 N.T. Insufficient values for a positive response, even though there is a biddable spade suit. If opener rebids 3♡, raise to 4♡.

9B. Your partner deals and opens 2♣. What would you respond?

	1. ♠ K 9 7 2	2. ♠ J 9	3. ♠ K J 9
	♡ K 6 4	♡ K 9 7 2	♡ K Q 7 6 2
	◇ Q 9 3 2	◇ K 9 8	◇ A 6 2
	♣ K 7	♣ Q J 8 4	♣ 8 4

Answers:
Bid (2 pts.)   Reason (3 pts.)

1. 4♠   The immediate double raise shows good trump support, 10-12 pts., but *no* ace or void.

2. 3 N.T. The approximate equivalent of a limit bid of 2 N.T. facing a one-level opening, though facing a Strong Two it denies a biddable suit and, by inference, denies a trump fit good enough for a raise to the four-level.

3. 3♠   The spade support is more than adequate for a suit good enough to open at the two-level. The single raise, besides agreeing the trump suit, also promises at least one ace or void.

10A. Your partner deals and opens 2♡. What would you respond?

1. ♠ 9 7	2. ♠ 9 7 4	3. ♠ —
♡ —	♡ 10 3	♡ K 9 7 4
◇ A K Q J 10 8 7 5	◇ 8 4	◇ K 7 5 3
♣ 9 6 4	♣ K Q 9 8 6 4	♣ K J 8 6 3

Answers:
Bid (2 pts.)   Reason (3 pts.)

1. 4◇ This is a jump bid in a forcing situation (as 2♡ is a one-round force). It shows a solid self-supporting trump suit for which no fit or support is needed.

2. 2 N.T. Though the clubs would just be worth showing if this could be done without raising the bidding level, a 'positive' response would make the sequence forcing to game.

3. 3♡ A single raise promises a good trump fit and at least one first-round control—in this case the spade void.

10B. Your partner deals and opens 2♠. What would you respond?

1. ♠ 9 7	♠ 9 3	3. ♠ Q J 9 7
♡ K 10 8 4	♡ 8 7	♡ A K Q J 10 9 3
◇ A 7 6	◇ K Q J 10 8 6 5	◇ 8
♣ 9 8 7 5	♣ K 9	♣ 7

Answers:
Bid (2 pts.)   Reason (3 pts.)

1. 2 N.T. Even with 1½ Q.T. it is better to give a negative response on the first round. You can't support spades or bid a red suit, and 3 N.T. would deny an ace. (A 2♡ opening you would, of course, have raised to 3♡.)

2. 3◇ A natural bid in you own good suit which by inference denies ability to support partner's suit.

3. 4 N.T. With this superb spade fit all you need to know for a slam is whether you are missing one or two aces. If partner has only one (unlikely) you can stop in 5♠.

11A. Your partner deals and opens 3♡. What would you respond?

1. ♠ A K J 6	2. ♠ A K Q J 7 6	3. ♠ K J 10 9 7 6 4
♡ K Q 3	♡ 5	♡ 8
◇ A Q J 6 2	◇ K Q J 10	◇ 9 5
♣ 7	♣ 10 7	♣ A Q 4

Answers:

Bid (2 pts.)   Reason (3 pts.)

1.   4◇   A change-of-suit response to an opening pre-emptive bid, if it is one below game level, is a one-round force. In principle a minor suit response should be taken as a slam invitation in the suit opened and a major suit response as a game invitation which may be raised on as good as Q-x in support.

2.   4♠   Not being slam-minded the best bid is an immediate 4♠ which opener can hardly misunderstand.

3.   No   Never 'rescue' into a suit which you have no assurance
       Bid   will be better than partner's. The thing he's *least* likely to hold is good spade support!

11B. Your partner deals and opens 3♡. What would you respond?

1. ♠ A 10 7	2. ♠ 9	3. ♠ A Q 10 7 6
♡ J 9 4	♡ Q 9 8 6 2	♡ K 10 7
◇ A Q 6	◇ Q 8 4	◇ 8
♣ K Q 10 9	♣ J 7 5 3	♣ A Q 7 3

Answers:

Bid (2 pts.)   Reason (3 pts.)

1.   4♡   Even facing a Weak Three you must have at least a play for game with 3½ honour tricks. Raise partner to 4♡.

2.   4♡   This is not because you have a hope of making it but to make it as difficult as possible for your left-hand opponent to come into the auction. Partner's Weak Three plus your 5 pts. won't go far in defence!

3.   4♡   Not quite the power to be slam-minded and not much point in suggesting a spade game contract with such excellent support for hearts. Reverse your heart and diamond holdings, though, and you should bid 3♠.

12A. Your partner deals and opens 2♣. What would you respond?

	1. ♠ Q 10 8 7 4	2. ♠ Q 10 8 7 4	3. ♠ 9 3
	♡ A 6 2	♡ 7 6 2	♡ A K Q J 10 8 5
	◊ K J 4	◊ K 9 3	◊ 7 2
	♣ 8 3	♣ 8 3	♣ 8 5

Answers:
Bid (2 pts.)   Reason (3 pts.)

1. 2♠ A positive response showing your biddable suit in a hand which contains not only the requirement of one ace and one king, but the other of any 8 pts.

2. 2◊ A negative response denying the values to make any constructive bid at this stage.

3. 3♡ A forcing situation is in being here, so the jump bid shows a solid and self-supporting trump suit. Even if partner has a heart void you can play in a heart slam without any misgivings.

12B. Your partner deals and opens 2♣. What would you respond?

	1. ♠ K 10 8	2. ♠ K J 8	3. ♠ A 10
	♡ J 9 7 4	♡ 7 6 2	♡ K J 9 4
	◊ Q J 6	◊ A 10 9 6 5	◊ Q J 6 3
	♣ K 7 2	♣ 8 3	♣ 7 6 2

Answers:
Bid (2 pts.)   Reason (3 pts.)

1. 2 N.T. A positive response showing at least eight honour points and no biddable suit.

2. 3◊ As 2◊ would be the negative response, it is necessary to show positive values with a biddable diamond suit by going to 3◊ which is not, of course, a jump bid in any other sense of the word.

3. 2♡ This is a perfectly biddable suit in a hand with good —extremely good—positive values. You would willingly bid it as the one-level, and can do so now.

NO-TRUMP BIDDING
The Basic Rules

EXAMPLES of no-trump opening bids, both weak and strong, were given in Section I, so here we concern ourselves with responding to these openings and to the possible development of the subsequent auction.

As pointed out on p. 10, the strength of an opening no-trump is a matter of partnership agreement, and from then onwards, many of the responses are a question of simple arithmetic, based on the table below. These counts are, of course, arbitrary, and as your experience develops you will learn to give due weight to suit length, the quality of controls and intermediates, and so on. Note too that the minimum of 25 pts. shown as necessary for a game in no-trumps is very conservative, and many a successful game can be made on less, particularly as declarer-skill develops.

No-trump Contracts

25-26 pts. between two evenly-balanced hands for a game.
33-34 pts. between two evenly-balanced hands for a Little Slam.
37 pts. between two evenly-balanced hands for a Grand Slam.

Suit Contracts

26 pts. with a trump fit for a major suit game.
28-29 pts. with a trump fit for a minor suit game.
31-33 pts. with a trump fit for a Little Slam.
37 pts. with a trump fit for a Grand Slam.

1. *Direct Raises of No-Trump Openings*

1 N.T. Weak (12-14) pts.)	Raise to 2 N.T. on 11 or a poor quality 12 pts., invitational but *not* forcing. Raise direct to 3 N.T. on 12+ pts.
1 N.T. Strong (15-17 pts.)	Raise to 2 N.T. on 8-9 pts., invitational but not forcing. Raise direct to 3 N.T. on 10 pts.

2 N.T. (20-22 pts.)	Raise to 3 N.T. on 4-5 pts. or even on 3 pts. and a five-card suit.
1 N.T. Weak 1 N.T. Strong	Raise to 4 N.T. quantitatively and invitationally if the combined minimum count is 31 pts.
2 N.T.	Raise to 6 N.T. if the combined minimum count is 33-34 pts. and cannot reach 37 pts.
	Raise direct to 7 N.T. if the combined minimum count is 37 or more pts.
	Raise to 5 N.T. if the combined minimum count is 35 pts. and a maximum count in the opening hand may bring it to the Grand Slam requirements of 37 pts. This opening demands a rebid of 6 N.T. on a minimum hand and 7 N.T. on a maximum.

2. Suit Take-Out of No-Trump Opening

The values needed depend on the known strength of the opening no-trump, as a hand worth only a weak take-out facing 12-14 pts. may be worth a game facing 15-17 pts. Whatever the strength of the opening bid:

2♦, 2♥, 2♠	Shows a weak unbalanced hand better fitted for a suit contract—a five-card suit or longer and no game ambitions.
3♥, 3♠	A game force showing the values to play in game, either suit or no-trumps.
3♣, 3♦	Slam invitation in the minor.
4♥, 4♠, 5♣, 5♦	Pre-emptive shut-out bids based on very unbalanced hands with at least a seven-card suit.
2♣	Conventional fit-finding bid of unrevealed strength showing interest in a major suit contract (see below).
4♣	Conventional 'Gerber' request to show aces. In response, 4♦ = no ace: 4♥ = one ace: 4♠ = two aces: 4 N.T. = three aces. A 5♣ rebid then asks for kings on the same "step" scale.

3. 2♣ Response to 1 N.T.—Opener's rebids and Responder's Actions

2♦	Rebid by opener, denies a four-card major holding, irrespective of opener's diamonds or his point count.
1 NT—2♣ 2♦—2♥	Responder may now, according to strength, make a weak take-out, or even pass 2♦ if that seems wisest. Alternatively responder may convert to 2 N.T. or 3 N.T. according to his values. He may also repeat
1 NT—2♣ 2♦—3♣	clubs at the three-level, which shows a long weak club suit, and no interest in a game contract.

1 NT—2♣
2◇—3♣ A jump rebid by responder is now highly invitational but not forcing, showing a hand on which he is doubtful about going on to game once a four-card fit for his major suit is known to be missing.

1 NT—2♣
2◇—3◇ Responder's 3◇ rebid asks for opener's *better* major. Opener should show the longer of the two and, if both are of equal length, the stronger.

1 NT—2♣
2♡ In response to the 2♣ bid, opener should show a four-card major suit if held. With both he should bid hearts first.* Responder may now, according

1 NT—2♣
2♠—3♠
or 4♠
or 2 NT
or 3 NT to his strength and whether or not the hoped-for fit has been discovered, pass the two-level bid, raise invitationally to the three-level, raise direct to the suit game, or convert to 2 or 3 N.T. Responder must never bid 2♣ in the first place unless, whatever opener replies, he himself has a sensible rebid available. (*Alternative treatment)

1 NT—2♣
2♡—3◇ S.I.D. convention agreeing major suit fit but offering opener choice of 3 N.T. or 4 of a major contract. (Stayman In Doubt.) No ruffing values.

4. Suit Take-Out of 2 N.T. Opening and Opener's Rebids

2 NT—3♡
or 3♠ There is no immediate weak take-out of an opening 2 N.T. and opener must rebid 3 N.T. or 4♡ or 4♠ as appropriate.

2 NT—4♡
or 4♠ A mild slam try on a hand which must be played in the suit named. Opener judges whether to pass or try again.

2 NT—3♣ Requests opener to show four-card suits in ascending order and, if his only four-card suit is clubs, to rebid 3 N.T. (The 'Baron' Convention.)

2 NT—3◇
3♡ 'Flint' request to opener to transfer to 3♡ which responder can either pass (weak take-out) or 'correct' to 3♠ if that is his long weak suit.

2 NT—3◇
3♠ or
3 NT Opener can occasionally elect to force a game contract with a *maximum* hand. With a very strong heart fit, he rebids 3♠ which responder can pass or convert to hearts at the four-level or, with a strong fit for both majors, opener can force responder to select his suit at the four-level by bidding 3 N.T.

2 NT—3◇	Responder can show a genuine diamond suit and
3♡—3 NT	mild slam ambitions by taking out opener's forced response into 3 N.T.
2 NT—4♣	'Gerber' as over 1 N.T.

Note:

Exactly the same sequences are used when the bidding has started 2♣—2◇—2 NT, except that responder must allow for the greater announced strength of his partner's opening bid (23-24 pts.).

5. *Other No-Trumps Openings*

3 N.T.	This is a tactical bid based on a long solid minor suit. Pass unless you have something obviously better to bid. It is not an opening bid to concern learners who would do better to open suitable hands with a pre-emptive bid in the minor suit concerned.
4 N.T.	A conventional opening bid requiring responder to show aces immediately on the following scale: With no ace, 5♣: with the ♣A, 6♣ with the ◇A, ♡A, or ♠A, five of the suit in which the ace is held; with two aces, 5 N.T.

NO TRUMP BIDDING

Exercises

♠♡♣◇♠♡♣◇♠♡♣◇♠♡♣◇♠♡♣◇♠♡♣◇♠♡♣◇

No. 1 ♠ J 9 5
    ♡ Q 4
    ◇ Q 8 7 3
    ♣ K J 7 4

Your partner deals and opens 1 N.T. What would you respond if the agreed strength were 12-14 pts., and what if it were 15-17 pts.?

Answer: On evenly balanced hands when no question of taking out into a suit arises, the only point for responder to consider is the combined strength of the two hands. If this reaches 25-26 pts. he should raise direct to 3 N.T. If he is doubtful, that is, if opener needs to have his maximum rather than his minimum for game values, then responder should raise invitationally to 2 N.T.

Here, with 9 pts. to add to opener's known maximum of 14 pts. it is impossible for game values to be held and responder should pass. If, on the other hand, the known opening values held were 15-17 pts., this becomes a joint minimum of 24 pts., and responder should raise invitationally to 2 N.T.

Many an expert player is happy to be in 3 N.T. on a combined 24 pts., but as learners you would do well to work on the higher count.

(Bids: No Bid and 2 N.T.)

No. 2 ♠ A Q 7 4
    ♡ J 9 5
    ◇ Q 8 6
    ♣ Q 7 2

Your partner deals and opens 1 N.T. What would you respond if the agreed strength were 12-14 pts., and what if it were 15-17 pts.?

Answer: This is another exercise in simple arithmetic. Facing a known minimum of 12 pts. responder can see a certain 23 pts. between the combined hands but to reach game values opener must hold his maximum of 14pts., or at any rate a 'good quality' 13 pts., so responder should raise invitationally to 2 N.T.

Facing a 15-17 pt. no-trump responder knows that the combined minimum is 26 pts., so he should raise direct to 3 N.T. He must not leave the onus on opener by bidding only 2 N.T., as opener, with his minimum of 15 pts., would pass.

(Bids: 2 N.T. and 3 N.T.)

No. 3　♠ Q 8 3　　　　'Your partner deals and opens 1 N.T.
　　　　♡ A Q 9　　　　What would you respond if the
　　　　◇ A 7 4　　　　agreed strength were 12-14 pts., and
　　　　♣ J 6 5 3　　　what if it were 15-17 pts.?

Answer : With 13 pts. facing a minimum of 12 pts. there is no need to look further than an immediate raise to 3 N.T. The combined count cannot be less than 25 pts., nor more than 27 pts., not up to slam requirements but comfortably at the game level.

When the combined count is a good deal higher than game requirements, responder must next make sure it isn't up to the slam level. Even facing the maximum of 17 pts. in a strong no-trump, the combined total cannot be more than 30 pts., insufficient on which to bid a slam. Again, responder should simply bid 3 N.T.

(Bids : 3 N.T. in either case.)

No. 4　♠ K J 7　　　　Your partner deals and opens 1 N.T.
　　　　♡ A Q 7　　　　What would you respond if the
　　　　◇ K 9 8 4　　　agreed strength were 12-14 pts., and
　　　　♣ A Q 3　　　　what if it were 15-17 pts.?

Answer : 19 pts. facing a minimum of 12 add up to 31, below the requirements for a slam on two evenly balanced hands. But if partner has 14 . . . ? Bid a quantitative, *not* conventional 4 N.T., which your partner will understand as an invitation to go to 6 N.T. if his hand is maximum strength. With a minimum he will pass.

Facing a 15-17 pt. no-trump, the combined minimum must be 34 pts., within the 33-35 pt. range which makes a Little Slam contract a good proposition, so the only other question is whether a Grand Slam should be bid. For this there should be a minimum of 37 pts. between the two hands, and your 19 pts. added to your partner's maximum of 17 pts, cannot be more than 36 pts. So here responder should just bid 6 N.T. with no beating about the bush.

(Bid : 4 N.T. and 6 N.T.)

No. 5   ♠ A 7   Your partner deals and opens 1 N.T.
       ♡ K J 8 7 5 4   What would you respond if the
       ◇ 9 5   agreed strength were 12-14 pts., and
       ♣ J 7 2   what if it were 15-17 pts.?

Answer : Facing a maximum of 14 pts., you would need to find
every adverse card lying 'right' to make a game, and it is also
obvious that the hand should be played in hearts, not in no-trumps.
Bid 2♡, a weak take-out, which opener is expected to pass.

Facing a strong no-trump, which contains a known minimum
of 15 pts., you want to be in a game contract but would prefer
hearts to no-trumps. Bid 3♡, a forcing-to-game bid, and opener
will either convert to 3 N.T. or raise to 4♡. He has one other
possibility, which you will meet in No. 8.

(Bids: 2♡ and 3♡.)

No. 6   ♠ 10 9 7 5 3 2   Your partner deals and opens 1 N.T.
       ♡ 9 6 2   What would you respond if the
       ◇ J 10 3   agreed strength were 12-14 pts., and
       ♣ 7   what if it were 15-17 pts.?

Answer : It makes no difference whether partner's opening no-
trump is weak or strong—this hand won't run to a game contract,
and it isn't even likely to produce a plus score unless it can be
played in spades. In either case, therefore, take out into 2♠.

Many players still have the idea that a weak take-out is for use
facing a weak no-trump only. This is quite incorrect, as it doesn't
matter whether the opening hand is weak or strong as long as
responder is sure of two things, first that the combined hands won't
produce a game and second, that they are likely to play better in
a suit than in no-trumps. Note also that weak take-out bids can
be made in spades, hearts, and diamonds, but not in clubs which,
as you will see in later examples, is used conventionally.

(Bids: 2♠ in either case.)

No. 7   ♠ A 9 6 4   Being not vulnerable you open
        ♡ J 10   1 N.T. as dealer. What would you
        ♢ K J 6 2   rebid if partner responds:
        ♣ K 7 4   a) 2♡: b) 2 N.T.: c) 3♠: and
                                 d) 3♡?

Answers: (a) Partner's 2♡ is a weak take-out, and even though it has come in your own poorest suit you must respect his decision and pass.

(b) 2 N.T. is invitational, an invitation which, on your minimum hand, you reserve your right to refuse. Pass.

(c) 3♠ is game-forcing, leaving you to choose between 3 N.T. and 4♠. With this excellent spade fit the latter is the correct choice.

(d) 3♡ is also game-forcing, but warn your partner of your poor, no better than a doubleton, fit by rebidding 3 N.T. Don't panic if he removes to 4♡.

                     (Bids: No Bid, No Bid, 4♠, and 3 N.T.)

No. 8   ♠ K 8 7   Again not vulnerable, you open
        ♡ Q 10 6 3   1 N.T. What would you rebid if
        ♢ K J 9   partner responds:
        ♣ A J 7   a) 2♢: b) 2 N.T.: c) 3♡ ?

Answers: (a) Even with your maximum of 14 pts. you must respect partner's decision and pass.

(b) 2 N.T. is, as you know, invitational, and this time you have no hesitation in accepting the invitation to go on to 3 N.T.

(c) Here we meet a new situation. Responder has made a game force, at the same time saying that he fancies a heart contract. You have a maximum for your bid—in fact ½ pt. over—and, too, your best suit is hearts. In such circumstances, when you would in any case raise to 4♡, make an 'advance cue-bid' of 4♣ on the way. This shows trump agreement, a maximum opening no-trump, and the ace of the cue-bid suit.

                       (Bids: No Bid, 3 N.T., and 4♣.)

No. 9   ♠ 10 9 8 5 4   Your partner deals and opens 1 N.T.
        ♡ J 9 6 5 3   What would you respond if the
        ◇ J 8   strength were 12-14 pts., and what
        ♣ 7   if it were 15-17 pts.?

Answer: Clearly this hand won't run to a game contract whether opener is strong, let alone only holding 12-14 pts., so whichever you know he has, you would cope in the same way. You would prefer to play in spades or hearts, but who are you to guess which will fit his hand better? *Ask* him by bidding a conventional 2♣.

2♣ is a request to opener to show any major four-card holding. With both he should bid the hearts first and with neither he should rebid 2◇ irrespective of his actual diamond holding. Responder can now judge whether to pass at the two level, raise the suit invitationally to the three-level, bid a suit game contract direct or, if the response is not what he wanted to hear, convert to 2 or 3 N.T., according to strength. The one essential for responder is that, before he bids 2♣, he should make sure he has a sensible course of action he can take on the next round. Here he would pass a 2♡ or 2♠ rebid, or convert 2◇ to 2♡, his slightly better suit.

(Bids: 2♣ in either case.)

No. 10 ♠ Q 9 7 4   Your partner deals and opens 1 N.T.
        ♡ K 6 3 2   What would you respond if the
        ◇ 10   strength were 12-14 pts., and what
        ♣ Q J 4 2   if it were 15-17 pts.?

Answer: Here's a case in point where, facing a 12-14 pt. no-trump, there is nothing sensible you can do on the next round if, in reply to 2♣ from you, partner rebids 2◇. Your two major suits are neither good enough to 'rescue' yourself into one of them at the two-level, and you haven't enough points to convert to 2 N.T which would tell partner you could have bid 2 N.T. in the first place. All you can do, therefore, is to pass.

Facing a strong no-trump you *could* raise 1 N.T. to 2 N.T. invitationally, so you can take your chance to bid 2♣ to ask partner if he has four spades or hearts. If he says yes, you can raise invitationally to three of the suit, and if he says no by bidding 2◇ you can convert to 2 N.T.

(Bids: No Bid and 2♣.)

No. 11 ♠ K Q 9 8
      ♡ A Q 7 4 3
      ◇ 9
      ♣ 7 4 2

Your partner deals and opens 1 N.T. What would you respond if the strength were 12-14 pts., and what if it were 15-17 pts.?

Answer : In either case you would respond 2♣ because it is clear that you would prefer this hand to be played in hearts or spades, particularly if partner has four cards in either. Notice that the hand contains a perfectly sensible rebid whatever partner responds, even 2◇.

If opener rebids either 2♡ or 2♠, showing a four-card suit, then whether his opening no-trump were weak or strong, you would put him to four in that suit.

As you learned in No. 9, responder can use this 2♣ bid on any strength of hand provided he wants to investigate a major suit fit and that he has a sensible rebid available, whatever the answer to his question.

(Bids: 2♣ in either case.)

No. 12 ♠ J 9 7 2
      ♡ 10 8 6 4
      ◇ J 7 6 5 3
      ♣ —

Your partner deals and opens 1 N.T. What would you respond if the strength were 12-14 pts., and what if it were 15-17 pts.?

Answer : This is another hand on which, whatever the strength of the opening no-trump, two things are clear, firstly it won't run to a successful game contract, and secondly, it is quite horrible for play in no-trumps. The final question, then, is whether or not it contains a sensible course of action if you bid 2♣ to see whether opener has a four-card major suit, and the answer to this too is yes.

If opener shows either four hearts or four spades by his rebid you will pass, knowing that he is likely to be far happier in a four-four trump fit than in no-trumps. If he bids 2◇ to deny a four card major, then again you will pass. The less length he has in hearts and spades, the better fit he is likely to have for diamonds, and your pass will only be leaving him in the suit in which you could have made a weak take-out in the first place.

(Bids: 2♣ in either case.)

No. 13 ♠ K J 6   You deal and open 1 N.T. (12-14
       ♡ Q 9 6 2   pts.), to which partner responds 2♣.
       ♢ Q J 5   What would you rebid?
       ♣ A 7 4

Answer : Partner's 2♣ is a conventional request to you to show whether or not you have a four-card major suit, so your rebid is 2♡.

Had you held four spades instead of four hearts you would have rebid 2♠ and with both majors containing four cards you would show hearts first, which is the modern method of handling this type of holding.

Had you held an extra two points you would not have opened 1 N.T. on this hand unless the agreed strength were 15-17 pts. In that case your response to a 2♣ bid from partner would have been exactly the same—these bids operate over any agreed strength of 1 N.T. opening.

(Bid: 2♡.)

No. 14 ♠ Q 10 6   You deal and open 1 N.T. to which
       ♡ A 9 7   your partner responds 2♣. You
       ♢ Q J 5   correctly rebid 2♢ to deny a four-
       ♣ K J 7 2   card major suit and he now bids
                       3♡. What would you bid?

Answer : Obviously partner's 2♣ was bid in the hope that he would find you with a four-card heart fit. Now that you have said you can't oblige he is doubtful about going on to 4♡ and is *asking* your opinion. In other words, his 3♡ is now highly invitational, but not forcing.

With your good opening no-trump (13½ pts. is very far from minimum) and ♡A-x-x, an excellent fit, accept the invitation by raising him to 4♡.

(Bid: 4♡.)

No. 15 ♠ K J 8
&heart; Q 9 6
♦ Q 7
♣ A J 9 6 5

There is no law against opening 1 N.T. with a five-card suit, particularly when it is a minor. You open 1 N.T. and partner responds 2♣. What would you rebid?

Answer: Until responder takes some further action to clarify his bid, 2♣ must be taken as a request to show any four-card major suit held. Lacking one, the rebid is 2♦ which, as you can see, bears no relation to the actual diamond holding or, for that matter, to anything else in the hand. So the correct rebid here is 2♦.

Don't take it upon yourself to pass in this situation just because you have a weakish hand and a five-card club suit. Your partner may be good enough to put you straight to 3 N.T. except that he has thought it wiser to investigate your major suit holdings first.

(Bid: 2♦.)

No. 16 ♠ Q J 9 6 5 3
&heart; 7
♦ K 6 3
♣ 8 4 2

Your partner deals and opens 1 N.T. (12-14 pts.). What would you respond and what difference would it make if you held six clubs instead of six spades?

Answer: Holding the hand as it is above, with six spades, you would make a weak take-out into 2♠, which would be passed by your partner. He will understand that you have a weak hand which you think will play better in spades than in no-trumps.

If your suit were clubs instead of spades you would still not want to let partner play in no-trumps but, if you understood the previous quizzes, you will realise that 2♣ is conventional and so can't be used as a weak take-out bid.

The way to deal with this is to bid 2♣ and, when partner makes his conventional response, either showing or denying a four-card major, take out again into 3♣, from which he will understand that your only asset is a long weak club suit.

(Bids: 2♠ and 2♣.)

No. 17 ♠ A Q 7   Your partner deals and opens 1 N.T.
         ♡ K J 8 2   What would you respond if the
         ◇ A Q J   agreed strength were 12-14 pts., and
         ♣ A K 5   what if it were 15-17 pts.?

Answer : Your 24 pts. plus partner's known minimum of 12 pts. comes to a total of 36, amply good enough for a Little Slam. But if you put him direct to 6 N.T. he will certainly pass even if, as is possible, he has his maximum of 14 pts., though you would have an odds-on chance of making a Grand Slam. Bid a *conventional* 5 N.T., which *orders* partner to bid 6 N.T. even on the barest minimum for his bid, and asks him to bid 7 N.T. on a maximum. The one thing he mustn't do, of course, is to pass 5 N.T.!

Facing a 15-17 pt. no-trump you know that there can't be more than one knave missing from the combined hands, so bid a direct 7 N.T. without even consulting partner on the way.

(Bids : 5 N.T. and 7 N.T.)

No. 18 ♠ A   Your partner deals and opens 1 N.T.
         ♡ K Q J 10 6 5 4 3 (12-14 pts.), What would you re-
         ◇ A 7 2   spond?
         ♣ 5

Answer : It's well within the bounds of possibility that partner's weak no-trump opening contains no aces, in which case you might as well play in a comfortable 4♡. But if he has even one ace, you want to play in a Little Slam, and if he has two, in a Grand Slam contract.

Bid 4♣, the conventional 'Gerber' request, which is used in place of 'Blackwood' when the opening bid has been either 1 N.T. or 2 N.T. The responses are, to show no ace, 4◇—in which case you would simply convert to 4♡—4♡ to show one ace, when you would convert to 6♡, and 4♠ to show two aces which you would convert to 7♡, (7 N.T. at duplicate). Using this convention, any rebid *other than* 5♣, which asks for kings on the same step principle, is the 4♣ bidder's decision as to the best final contract, and should not be disturbed.

(Bid : 4♣.)

No. 19 ♠ K J 10 7 6   Your partner deals and opens 1 N.T.
       ♡ A Q J 9 3   (12-14 pts.). You correctly bid 2♣
       ◇ 7 5   to which he replies 2◇. What would
       ♣ 8   you rebid?

Answer :   Your 2♣ response was, of course, asking for any four-card major held by your partner, but he has replied that he has none. In spite of this, however, you feel sure the hand will play better in spades or hearts, which ever fits his hand best. After all, having opened 1 N.T. he cannot have less than a doubleton in both, and may have three in both or one of them.

Bid a conventional 3◇ which requests opener to show you his *longer* major. That is, if he has a three-card and a two-card suit, he bids the three-card suit. If both are of equal length he should bid the stronger. Whichever he chooses, you will raise him to game.

(Bid : 3◇.)

No. 20 ♠ Q J 10 6   Your partner deals and opens 1 N.T.
       ♡ Q J 9 8 5 4   (12-14 pts.). You respond 2♣ in the
       ◇ A 8   hope of finding a four-card fit but
       ♣ 7   opener rebids 2◇. What would you
                       bid?

Answer :   Had opener bid 2♡ or 2♠ you would have put him straight to game in what you know to be a good fit. He has, however, denied a four-card major which makes you very much less certain that a game is 'on', even with this highly distributional hand.

Over 2◇ bid 3♡, not a mere 2♡ which would now be a weak take-out which he would pass. 3♡ is non-forcing but highly invitational and opener will raise to 4♡ if he possibly can or, perhaps, convert to 3 N.T. if the hearts are his weakest suit.

Such hands are very difficult to judge correctly, and you may be missing a game if you fail to jump direct to 4♡. Make one of your queens into a king and that would be your correct rebid.

(Bid : 3♡.)

No. 21   ♠ 9   Your partner deals and opens 1 N.T.
       ♡ A J 10 8 6 5 2   (12-14 pts.). What would you re-
       ◇ Q 8 5 3   spond?
       ♣ 6

Answer: It is pointless to beat about the bush in any way here, specially as opener's possible minimum of 12 pts. added to your 7 pts. makes only 19, leaving the balance of 21 for your opponents. Your left-hand opponent may have an equally distributional hand, and you want to make it as difficult as you can for him to show it.

Bid an immediate pre-emptive 4♡, making it impossible for him to come into the auction below the four-level in spades or the five level in a minor.

A similar pre-emptive jump to the five-level in a minor can also be made with a bit of added length or strength to compensate for the higher contract. Apart from obstructing the opposition, such hands have an excellent chance of making a successful contract just on their distribution.

(Bid: 4♡.)

No. 22   ♠ 10 9 5   Your partner deals and opens 2 N.T.
       ♡ Q 10 7 4   (20-22 pts.). What would you re-
       ◇ K 8 3   spond?
       ♣ 9 5 2

Answer: Though you would pass a 1 N.T. opening, either weak or strong, without a moment's hesitation, when partner opens 2 N.T. you know he has a minimum of 20 pts. The same arithmetic applies—with 25-26 pts. you want to be in game.

It's worth raising 2 N.T. to 3 N.T. even on 4 pts., especially if the hand contains good intermediates or a five-card suit. Here, counting your two tens, you have 6 pts., so raise to 3 N.T.

The rules for responding to 2 N.T. openings are somewhat different from those for responding to 1 N.T., and we shall be covering these for the remainder of this section.

(Bid: 3 N.T.)

No. 23 ♠ 8   Your partner deals and opens 2 N.T.
        ♡ Q J 10 8 6 4 3 2   (20-22 pts.).   What would you re-
        ◇ 9 3   spond?
        ♣ 5 4

Answer: There is no immediate weak take-out available when
partner opens 2 N.T., so if you decide you must play in a suit
rather than in no-trumps, you will first have to decide whether
you want to play at the three-level, at game level, or whether you
want to try for a slam. On this hand the suit length, even with only
three honour points, makes you want to play in 4♡. Take out
into 3♡, a game-forcing bid and, if partner rebids 3 N.T., take out
into 4♡.

Remember two important things here. Firstly, this is one of the
points of bidding on which there are two schools of thought, so
make sure you and your partner are using the same method so
that no misunderstandings crop up. Secondly, the same sequences
can be used if partner has opened 2♣ and, after a 2◇ response,
rebids 2 N.T. to show 23-24 pts.

(Bid: 3♡.)

No. 24 ♠ —   Your partner deals and opens 2 N.T.
        ♡ K Q 10 9 7 5 3   (20-22 pts.).   What would you re-
        ◇ K 7 6   spond?
        ♣ 7 5 4

Answer: Compared with No. 23 above, this time you immediately feel at least mildly interested in a slam. *Without* slam
ambitions you would take out into 3♡ and then convert a 3 N.T.
rebid to 4♡. With mild slam ambitions, bid 4♡ direct.

This method actually facilitates slam investigations as in a
sequence which starts, for instance, 2NT—3♡—3 NT or 4♡,
it may be difficult for either of the partnership to decide whether
or not to go on for a slam try. If slam interest is announced
immediately by responder, the onus is on opener, who now knows
he is facing a long suit and moderate strength.

(Bid: 4♡.)

No. 25 ♠ Q 9 7 5 4   Partner deals and opens 2 N.T.
      ♡ Q 8 7 3   (20-22 pts.). What would you re-
      ◇ J 10 8 4   spond?
      ♣ —

Answer : As already mentioned, had opener started with 2♣ to which you had responded 2◇, you would treat his 2 N.T. rebid in the same way except that you would allow for the known greater strength.

Here you would infinitely prefer a suit to a no-trump contract. As you could bid 2♣ over 1 N.T. to investigate for a four-card fit, so now you can bid 3♣ to investigate for *any* fit. When the opening bid has been at this higher level, 3♣ requests opener to show his four-card suits *in ascending order* and, if his only four-card suit is clubs, to rebid 3 N.T.

So bid 3♣ and if partner responds 3 N.T., you will know he has at least a four-card club suit and can let him play in 3 N.T. If he responds 3◇ (his lowest-ranking, not necessarily his only four-card suit) try 3♡ which he can raise, convert to 3 N.T., or himself show spades.

(Bid: 3♣.)

No. 26 ♠ A J 9   You deal and open 2 N.T., to which
      ♡ K Q J   partner responds 3♣. What would
      ◇ K J 9 3   you rebid, and would it make any
      ♣ A Q 7   difference if your diamond and club
                   holdings were reversed?

Answer : You don't at this stage know whether your partner has a possible slam (if he can find the fit he hopes for) in mind, or whether he thinks a suit contract rather than one in no-trumps will be safer. It is only up to you to answer the question he has asked which is what four-card suits you have.

As the hand is now you would respond 3◇ which is, as it happens, your only, not your lower ranking four-card suit and you would also bid 3◇ if you had either four hearts or four spades too, as you are required to bid your four-card suits in *ascending* order, (The 'Baron' Convention).

Reversing your minor suits would give you a four-card club suit only, and you would rebid 3 N.T. With another four-card suit besides clubs, you would rebid in that.

(Bids: 3◇ and 3 N.T.)

No. 27   ♠ 9   Your partner deals and opens 2 N.T.
        ♡ J 9 8 7 6 3   (20-22 pts.). What would you re-
        ◇ 10 7 5   spond?
        ♣ 5 4 2

Answer :   Compare this with No. 23, where you wanted to try for
a game in spite of the weakness in honour points. Here you are
far too weak to want to go as far as 4♡, but if you bid 3♡ this,
when partner has opened 2 N.T., is not a weak take-out. Partner
will rebid 3 N.T. or 4♡, when clearly the best contract is going
to be 3♡.

The solution here is to bid a conventional 'Flint' 3◇, requesting opener to make a transfer bid of 3♡, which you will pass. This
simple device gives you a means of getting out of a dangerous
no-trump contract into a far safer suit part-score contract.

                                             (Bid : 3◇.)

No. 28   ♠ J 9 8 7 6 3   Your partner deals and opens 2 N.T.
        ♡ 9   (20-22 pts.). What would you re-
        ◇ 10 7 5   spond?
        ♣ 5 4 2

Answer :   This is the same hand as No. 27 except that the major
suits are reversed, giving you long weak spades instead of hearts.
Bid 3◇, as you did before, and when your partner, as this requests,
transfers to 3♡, convert to 3♠ which, if he knows the convention,
he will pass.

Note, by the way, that if you hold a genuine diamond suit and
slam ambitions, the way to cope with this is to make the 3◇
response which opener will take as a request to transfer to 3♡
and then, when he does this, convert to 3 N.T. instead of accepting
the three-level contract. Partner should get the message.

                                             (Bid : 3◇.)

No. 29 ♠ K Q 9
      ♡ A Q 7
      ♢ K J 7 4
      ♣ A Q 10

You deal and open 2 N.T. (20-22 pts.), to which partner responds 3♢. What would you rebid, and what action would you take if he then bid 3 N.T.?

Answer : Simply follow partner's instructions, as his 3♢ response asks you to do, and make a transfer bid of 3♡. Most probably he has a long weak heart suit, so will then himself pass or, if his suit is spades, he will rebid 3♠—which you will pass.

Should he rebid 3 N.T. when you bid 3♡, he will be showing slam interest with a diamond contract in view. The least you can do is take the hint. Bid what must be a 'Blackwood' 4 N.T. and if by any chance he has no ace you can pass his 5♢ reply. If he has one ace, 6♢ must be a good proposition.

(Bids : 3♡ and 4 N.T.)

No. 30 ♠ A J 10
      ♡ A K 10 6
      ♢ A K 7 5
      ♣ K 8

You deal and open 2 N.T., to which your partner responds 3♢. What would you rebid, and would it make any difference if your two four-card suits were spades and diamonds or spades and hearts?

Answer : Generally, when partner asks for specific action it is wiser to heed his request, but exceptions do crop up. Here, for example, with a maximum opener and huge heart fit you feel that, even after his transfer request, you don't want to let him play in a mere 3♡. So make another conventional bid, a transfer to 3♠. If his suit is spades, as in No. 28, he will now pass, but if it is actually hearts, he will have to convert to this suit at the four level.

If the hearts and spades were exchanged, you would transfer to 3♡ as requested, but if partner then himself took out into 3♠ you would raise to 4♠. In the third case, with both major suits heavily held in a maximum hand, refuse the simple transfer and rebid 3 N.T., forcing partner to take himself out at game level into whichever suit he really holds.

(Bids : 3♠, 3♡, and 3 N.T.)

NO-TRUMP BIDDING
Competition Quiz

♠♡♣◇♠♡♣◇♠♡♣◇♠♡♣◇♠♡♣◇♠♡♣◇♠♡♣◇

In competition against another player, one should answer the three questions in the **A** set, and the other the three questions in the **B** set on each page.

1A. Your partner deals and opens 1 N.T. (12 -14 pts.). What would you respond?

1. ♠ K 9 7	2. ♠ K 9 7	3. ♠ K 9 7
♡ Q 3 2	♡ Q 3 2	♡ Q 3 2
◇ Q 7 5 4	◇ Q 7 5 4	◇ K 10 7 4
♣ A 6 3	♣ Q 6 3	♣ A 6 3

Answers:
Bid (2 pts.)   Reason (3 pts.)

1. 2 N.T.   Your combined count cannot be less than 23 pts. and may be up to the 25 needed for game if opener has 14, not his minimum of 12 pts. Bid an *invitational* 2 N.T.

2. No Bid   Even added to opener's possible maximum of 14 pts., the combined count can't be within the game range.

3. 3 N.T.   As the combined count can't be less than 24½ pts., this is well worth a direct raise to 3 N.T.

1B. Your partner deals and opens 1 N.T. (15-17 pts.). What would you respond?

1. ♠ Q 7 2	2. ♠ Q 7 3	3. ♠ Q 7 2
♡ K 9 7 2	♡ K 6 5 2	♡ K 6 5 2
◇ A 6 3	◇ Q 4 3	◇ Q 7 3
♣ Q 7 5	♣ Q 7 5	♣ 9 7 6

Answers:
Bid (2 pts.)   Reason (3 pts.)

1. 3 N.T.   The combined count cannot be less than 26 pts., ample for game, so bid it direct.

2. 2 N.T.   The invitational raise, in the hope that partner is better than minimum, in which case he will go to 3 N.T.

3. No Bid   The combined values can't reach game requirements, and you have no ambitions towards a suit contract anyway.

2A. Your partner deals and opens 1 N.T. (12-14 pts.). What would you respond?

1. ♠ Q 9 7 4	2. ♠ Q 9 7 4 3 2	3. ♠ 9 8
♡ K 8 3	♡ K 8	♡ Q 9 7 5 2
◇ J 9 7 5	◇ J 9 7 5	◇ 7 6
♣ 10 9	♣ 10	♣ K 9 7 3

Answers:
Bid (2 pts.)   Reason (3 pts.)

1. No Bid   Your hand is too weak to raise no-trumps or to suggest the alternative of a suit contract.

2. 2♠   This is an immediate weak take-out, which opener is expected to pass. Clearly this hand will be best played in a low spade contract, and not in no-trumps.

3. 2♡   Another weak take-out, even though you have only a five-card suit. An opening no-trump must contain at least a doubleton heart, probably to an honour, which will make 2♡ a safer contract than 1 N.T. with two worthless doubletons in the hand.

2B. Your partner deals and opens 1 N.T. (15-17 pts.). What would you respond?

1. ♠ K 9	2. ♠ A J 10 7	3. ♠ 9 8 7 5 4 3
♡ Q 7 3	♡ J 9 8	♡ —
◇ Q 9 8 7 6 3	◇ A 8 3	◇ J 9 7 4
♣ 8 4	♣ 10 9 8	♣ 10 9 8

Answers:
Bid (2 pts.)   Reason (3 pts.)

1. 2◇   It makes no difference that the opening no-trump is strong—this hand will play better in a low-level diamond contract, so make a weak take-out.

2. 3 N.T.   A very suitable hand to play in no-trumps and simple arithmetic tells you that this should be at game level.

3. 2♠   Another example of a weak take-out. Don't leave partner to struggle in 1 N.T. when you may even make 2♠!

3A. Your partner deals and opens 1 N.T. (15-17 pts.). What would you respond?

1. ♠ K J 8 6 3 2	2. ♠ 8 7	3. ♠ A Q 7
♡ J 9 5	♡ 10 9 5	♡ K Q 6
◇ A 8	◇ A K J 9 7 4	◇ K J 10 6 5 4
♣ 10 6	♣ 10 6	♣ 4

Answers:

Bid (2 pts.)   Reason (3 pts.)

1. 3♠ You have ample points to want to play in game but would prefer this to be in spades, not no-trumps. If you bid 2♠ partner would pass, so make a game force of 3♠.

2. 3 N.T. You have no wish to play in 5◇ so it would be pointless to bid 3◇ on this hand. Bid what you think will be the best contract!

3. 3◇ This time you personally would prefer to play in a diamond contract, which you announce by the 3◇ game force. This hand may well run to a diamond slam.

3B. Your partner deals and opens 1 N.T. (12-14 pts.). What would you respond?

1. ♠ 10 8 4	2. ♠ 9	3. ♠ K J 8 6 3 2
♡ 9 7	♡ A Q 5	♡ J 9 5
◇ A K J 9 7 4	◇ K Q 7	◇ A 8
♣ 10 6	♣ K Q 10 6 5 4	♣ 10 6

Answers:

Bid (2 pts.)   Reason (3 pts.)

1. 2◇ Almost the same hand as **3A**, No. 2, but worth no more than a weak take-out when facing a maximum of 14 pts.

2. 3♣ Almost the same as **3A**, No. 3, and also worth a game forcing take-out of 3♣ which may well lead to a slam, so make the slam invitation of 3♣. If opener rebids 3 N.T., pass.

3. 2♠ The same hand as **3A**, No. 1, but worth no more than a weak take-out when facing a 12-14 pt. no-trump. Note the need for accuracy in all the no-trump opening bids, as the responses are based on a knowledge of the maximum and minimum values held.

4A. Your partner deals and opens 1 N.T. (15-17 pts.). What would you respond?

	1. ♠ K 7 6	2. ♠ K 7	3. ♠ K 7 6
	♡ A Q 5 2	♡ A Q 10 9 7 3	♡ A 10 8 7
	◇ A J 4	◇ A 6 4	◇ A 5 4
	♣ A K 8	♣ A K	♣ K J 6

Answers:

Bid (2 pts.)   Reason (3 pts.)

1. 5 N.T.   Your 21 pts. plus partner's minimum of 15 come to 36 pts., ample for a Little Slam. But if partner has his maximum there should be a good play for the Grand Slam. Bid 5 N.T. asking him to go to 6 N.T. with only 15 pts. and to 7 N.T. with more, or with suit length somewhere.

2.   4♣   Although a point weaker than No. 1, here there is a six-card heart suit. Get on immediately with the 'Gerber' investigation into aces and kings. 4♣ will surely get a 4♡ 'one ace' reply, and 5♣, if the answer is 5♠ showing both the missing kings, should lead you straight to 7♡ which may be a little safer than 7 N.T.

3. 3 N.T.   15 plus even 17 only come to 32 pts., not enough for a Little Slam without suit length, so just bid the game.

4B. Your partner deals and opens 1 N.T. (12-14 pts.). What would you respond?

	1. ♠ K J 6	2. ♠ A J 9 7 5 4 3	3. ♠ K J 5
	♡ A Q 5 2	♡ 6	♡ A J 7
	◇ A J 4	◇ 7 2	◇ A J 6
	♣ A K 8	♣ Q 6 3	♣ K Q J 4

Answers:

Bid (2 pts.)   Reason (3 pts.)

1. 6 N.T.   Your 22 pts. plus partner's 12 come to 34 pts., good enough for a Little Slam. But even if he has 14, it only comes to 36 pts., not enough for the Grand Slam, so bid 6 N.T. direct.

2.   4♠   A pre-emptive jump bid which partner is expected to pass. You might even make it!

3. 4 N.T.   Inviting opener to bid 6 N.T. if maximum or even with a good quality 13 pts. Otherwise he may pass.

5A. Your partner deals and opens 1 N.T. (12-14 pts.). What would you respond?

1. ♠ J 9 7 3	2. ♠ K 9 8 4	3. ♠ A K 7 4
♡ J 7 6 4 2	♡ J 10 8 6	♡ Q 3
◇ 9 3 2	◇ 5	◇ K 10 9
♣ 6	♣ Q 6 5 4	♣ J 6 4 2

Answers:

Bid (2 pts.)   Reason (3pts.)

1. 2♣ This hand will surely play better in hearts or spades if partner has a four-card fit for either. Bid 2♣ to ask him, and rebid 2♡ if he responds 2◇.

2. No   The essence of this 2♣ fit-finding bid is that you should
    Bid have some sensible bid to make on the next round, especially if you don't get the answer you hope for from partner. Here, if he bids 2◇ to deny a four-card major, what can you say next? So pass and hope for the best!

3. 2♣ With ample points to raise to 3 N.T. anyway, you would prefer a spade contract if partner has a four-card fit.

5B. Your partner has opened 1 N.T. (12-14 pts.), to which you have responded 2♣. What would you rebid if he now bid 2◇, and if instead he bid 2♡?

1. ♠ J 8 6 4 3	2. ♠ K 9 8 4	3. ♠ K 4 3
♡ J 10 9 5	♡ J 10 8 6	♡ A K 7 4
◇ 9 8 3	◇ 10 8 6 5 3	◇ Q 6 2
♣ 4	♣ —	♣ K 10 9

Answers:

Bids (1pt. each)   Reasons (1½pts. each)

1. 2♠ You could have made a weak take-out into 2♠ immediately except that you took your chance to ask whether opener had four cards in either major.

    No   You have discovered a four-four fit which is what you
    Bid hoped to do. Leave well alone.

2. No   You could have made a weak take-out into 2◇ except
    Bid that you asked first if he had a four-card major suit.
    No   Having found a four-card heart fit, again leave well
    Bid alone. No need to rescue yourself into diamonds.

3. 3 N.T. With ample points for the raise, put partner to game.
    3◇   Now you have a known four-four heart fit, offer partner the choice between 3 N.T. and 4♡ (S.I.D.).

6A. Your partner deals and opens 1 N.T. (12-14 pts.). What would you respond?

1. ♠ A J 10 7	2. ♠ J 8 5 3	3. ♠ K J 8 4
♡ A Q 9	♡ J 2	♡ A Q 2
◇ 10 7 4 2	◇ 8	◇ Q J 7
♣ 8 6	♣ Q 9 8 5 4 2	♣ Q 10 8

Answers:

Bid (2 pts.)   Reason (3 pts.)

1.   2♣   You would prefer to see this hand played in spades if partner has a four-card suit—ask him.

2.   2♣   Take your chance to ask if partner has a four-card spade suit. Both here and in No. 1 you have a sensible rebid if he replies 2◇ or 2♡.

3. 3 N.T.   An ideal hand for play in no-trumps and it can't make opener's up to slam requirements, so just bid game direct.

6B. You have responded 2♣ to partner's opening no-trump (12-14 pts.). What would you rebid if he now bid (a) 2◇, and (b) 2♠?

1. ♠ 8 6	2. ♠ J 8 5 3	3. ♠ K Q 10 6
♡ A J 10 7	♡ J 2	♡ 9 3 2
◇ A Q 9	◇ 8	◇ A J 9
♣ J 5 4 2	♣ Q 9 8 5 4 2	♣ K 7 5

Answers:

Bids (1 pt. each)   Reasons (1½ pts. each)

1. 3 N.T.   It's a pity opener hasn't got a four-card heart suit, but with 12½ pts. you must put him to game in no-trumps.

   3 N.T.   Partner's 2♠ denies four hearts as well, so he *won't* remove 3 N.T. to 4♡. At least you know he has a spade stop.

2.   3♣   Show that your original 2♣ was largely based on a long weak club suit.

     No   The known four-four spade fit is likely to be safest, so
     Bid   don't bother with your long clubs this time.

3. 3 N.T.   Partner has less than four spades or hearts, but you can't play below game level with 14 pts. in your hand.

     3◇   Having discovered the spade fit, offer partner the choice of 4♠ or 3 N.T. (S.I.D.).

7A. You deal and open 1 N.T. to which partner responds 2♣. What would you rebid?

1. ♠ K 10 9	2. ♠ K 10 9 4	3. ♠ K 10 9
♡ Q 8 7 5	♡ A Q 7 5	♡ Q 8 7
◇ Q J 8	◇ Q J 8	◇ Q J 8
♣ A Q 3	♣ J 6	♣ A Q 3 2

Answers:

Bid (2 pts.)   Reason (3 pts.)

1. 2♡   Answering the question you have been asked, and showing your four-card heart suit.

2. 2♡   Again answering the question, but showing the heart suit first. From this you will see that a rebid 2♠ denies four hearts, though a rebid of 2♡ does not deny four spades.

3. 2◇   It makes no difference that your hand is maximum for your 1 N.T. opening—just answer the question, which is whether or not you have a four-card major suit.

7B. Carrying the bidding of the same three hands a stage further, as opener, what would you bid next in each of these sequences?

1. 1 NT—2♣	2. 1 NT—2♣	3. 1 NT—2♣
2♡—3♡	2♠—2 NT	2◇—3♠
?	?	?

Answers:

Bid (2 pts.)   Reason (3 pts.)

1. 4♡   Responder is inviting a game now that he has discovered a four-four heart fit. With a maximum for your opening bid, accept the invitation.

2. 3♠   Presumably responder, who has now shown lack of interest in a heart fit, bid 2♣ in the hope that you would show spades. You *have* spades, as well as a hand which you are willing to play in 3 N.T. if you must, but you would prefer spades. Give partner the choice.

3. 4♠   Responder is strongly *inviting* a game contract in spite of your lack of a four-card spade suit. With your good quality opener and excellent three-card spade fit, go to 4♠.

8A. You deal and open 1 N.T. Partner responds 2♣ and you rebid 2◇. What would you bid if he next bid 3♡?

	1.	2.	3.
♠	K 7 2	K 7 2	K J 2
♡	Q 2	Q 2	Q 10 2
◇	K 8 7 5	K 8 7 5	K 8 7
♣	K J 6 2	A Q 6 2	A J 10 9

Answers:

Bid (2 pts.)   Reason (3 pts.)

1. No   Partner is strongly *inviting* a game contract, but nothing
    Bid   about your hand makes you want to accept.

2. 3 N.T. With a maximum opening and your weakest suit hearts,
          accept the invitation to bid a game, though in no-
          trumps.

3. 4♡   Again perfectly willing to accept the invitation to bid
          game, though this time, with excellent heart support.
          Tell partner this will suit you if it is what he prefers.

8B. On the same three hands as above, what would you, as opener, rebid in the following sequences?

1. 1 NT—3♡   2. 1 NT—4♣   3. 1 NT—3♠
   ?   ?   ?

Answers:

Bid (2 pts.)   Reason (3 pts.)

1. 3 N.T. As the 3♡ bid is forcing to game you have no option
          but to bid again. Deny better than a doubleton heart
          with 3 N.T.

2   4♡   This is, of course, the response to partner's 'Gerber'
          request to show aces. 4◇ would deny an ace, and 4♡
          shows one ace.

3. 4♣   Technically an advance cue bid in this position shows
          four-card trump agreement and a maximum no-trump
          with the ace of the suit bid. But a bit of common sense
          must be used—a player who can force in spades will be
          more than satisfied with ♠K-J-x in support, and with
          two tens you were really rather over strength for 1 N.T.
          in the first place.

9A. Your partner deals and opens 1 N.T. (15-17 pts.). What would you respond?

1. ♠ K 10 8 6 5	2. ♠ K 10 8 6 5	3. ♠ K 10 8 6 5
♡ Q J 9 8 4	♡ Q J 2	♡ Q J 9
◇ 7	◇ 7	◇ 7 3
♣ Q 2	♣ 10 9 6 3	♣ K 10 4

Answers:

Bid (2 pts.)   Reason (3 pts.)

1.   2♣   A less likely-looking hand for a happy no-trump contract would be difficult to find. Ask your partner if he can give you a fit for one of your majors.

2.   2♠   With an unsuitable shape for play in no-trumps and insufficient strength to bid 2 N.T. or 3♠, make a weak take-out into your five-card suit.

3.   3♠   You have the values to raise to game, but would prefer the hand to be played in spades, so say so.

9B

On hand No. 1 above what would you bid next in the sequence:
1 NT—2♣
   2◇—?

2. ♠ K 10 8 6 5
   ♡ Q J 7 2
   ◇ 7
   ♣ 10 9 6
   1 NT—2♣
      2♠—?

On hand No. 3 above what would you bid next in the sequence:
1 NT—3♠
3 NT—?

Answers:

Bid (2 pts.)   Reason (3 pts.)

1.   3◇   The hand is still highly unsuitable for play in no-trumps so you ask partner, with a conventional 3◇, to show his *better* major, i.e., three-card ahead of doubleton, and with two of equal length, to show the stronger.

2.   3♠   Although low in honour strength, this hand is distributionally strong, and if partner is maximum could easily run to game in the known 5-4 spade fit. Invite him.

3.   No   Partner already knows that you have a spade suit but
     Bid   this will be his poorest suit—no better than a doubleton. If he decides 3 N.T. will be better than 4♠, respect his decision.

10A. Your partner deals and opens 2 N.T. (20-22 pts.). What would you respond?

1. ♠ Q 10 8 3	2. ♠ Q 10 8 3	3. ♠ Q 9 8 6 5 4 3
♡ K 9 4	♡ K J 4	♡ 9 7
◇ 9 8 6	◇ K J 8 7	◇ A 6
♣ 8 5 3	♣ A 9	♣ 5 3

Answers:

Bid (2 pts.)   Reason (3 pts.)

1. 3 N.T. Facing a known minimum of 20 pts., you have ample for a raise to 3 N.T., and no reason to prefer a suit contract.

2. 6 N.T. Your 14 pts. plus opener's known minimum of 20 come to 34, good for a Little Slam, but even if he has 22 pts. it will make a very sticky proposition of the Grand Slam.

3.   3♠ There is no immediate weak take-out of a 2 N.T. opening, so any response commits the partnership to game. Also different authorities use these suit responses differently, so be careful you and your partner are on the same wave-length. Bid 3♠ and, if partner rebids 3 N.T., take out into 4♠.

10B. Your partner deals and opens 2 N.T. (20-22 pts.). What would you respond?

1. ♠ K 9 3	2. ♠ 7 4	3. ♠ Q 10 8 6
◇ A 7 5 4	♡ J 10 8 6 5 3	♡ K 9 7 2
◇ Q J 8	◇ 9 6 2	◇ J 8 5 4
♣ Q 10 7	♣ 8 4	♣ 7

Answers:

Bid (2 pts.)   Reason (3 pts.)

1. 4 N.T. Your 12 pts. plus partner's known minimum of 20 come to 32, but if he has his maximum of 22 pts. there should be a good chance of making a Little Slam. Bid a quantitative, *not* conventional, 4 N.T. inviting him to go to 6 N.T. if maximum.

2.   3◇ This is the 'Flint' conventional bid, asking partner to make a transfer bid of 3♡ which you intend to pass. This is your way of making a weak take-out into a major facing a 2 N.T. opening.

3.   3♣ This, facing 2 N. T., asks partner to show his four-card suits in *ascending* order, in the hope of finding a suit fit. If he has only one four-card suit, clubs, he will bid 3 N.T.

11A. You deal and open 2 N.T., to which partner responds 3♦. What would you rebid?

	1. ♠ A J 9 2	2. ♠ A 7	3. ♠ A Q J 10
	♡ A 10	♡ A Q J 10	♡ A 10 9 8
	◇ K Q J 7	◇ A K 8	◇ A K 8
	♣ A Q 6	♣ A 10 9 8	♣ A 7

Answers:
Bid (2 pts.)   Reason (3 pts.)

1.   3♡   Responder's 3◇ is a conventional request to you to transfer to 3♡, which he will probably pass. But if his long weak suit is spades, he will 'correct' to 3♠.

2.   3♠   Responder's 3◇ is still a request to you to transfer to 3♡ but with your maximum opener and strong heart fit you don't want him to play in a mere 3♡. Your 3♠ allows him to pass if spades is his suit, but otherwise he will have to 'correct' to 4♡.

3. 3 N.T.   With this powerful maximum you want the contract to reach game in either major, and 3 N.T. forces partner to pick the suit at the four-level.

11B. You deal and open 2 N.T., to which partner responds 3♣. What would you rebid?

Answers:
Bid (2 pts.)   Reason (3 pts.)

	1. ♠ A 10 9	2. ♠ A J 8 5	3. ♠ A J 8
	♡ A J 8 5	♡ A 10 9	♡ A 10 9
	◇ K Q 10	◇ A J	◇ A Q 5
	♣ A Q 6	♣ A Q 6 5	♣ A Q 6 5

1.   3♡   3♣ is 'Baron' requesting opener to show four-card suits in *ascending* order. (Some players use 'Stayman' as over 1 N.T., so make sure you and your partner understand each other!)

2.   3♠   With two four-card suits show the lower-ranking first unless it is clubs, which you can show later if expedient. 3♠, of course, denies a four-card red suit.

3. 3 N.T.   This rebid shows that the *only* four-card suit held is clubs.

12A. Your partner deals and opens 2♣, to which you respond
2♢. He then rebids 2 N.T. What would you bid next?

1. ♠ Q 9 4	2. ♠ Q 10 9 7 5	3. ♠ 9 5 3
♡ K 8 7 2	♡ J 9 8 6	♡ K 9 8 7 5 3
♢ 10 8 7	♢ 9 3	♢ Q 6 2
♣ 6 5 3	♣ 6 2	♣ 5

Answers:

Bid (2 pts.)   Reason (3 pts.)

1. 3 N.T.   Opener's rebid shows 23-24 pts. instead of the mere
20-22 of a 2 N.T. opening. You have ample to raise to
game.

2.   3♣   This bid is used in just the same way as facing a 2 N.T.
opening, that is, when you hope to find a suit rather
than a no-trump contract.

3.   3♡   This, of course, commits the partnership to game, but
you show that you would prefer the suit contract to
no-trumps. If opener rebids 3 N.T. you would be well
advised to take out into 4♡, a suit in which he is bound
to have at least a doubleton with an honour.

12B. Your partner deals and opens 2♣, to which you respond
2♢. He then rebids 2 N.T. What would you bid next?

1. ♠ 9 8 6 5 4 3	2. ♠ 9	3. ♠ J 9 4
♡ 7 4	♡ 8 7	♡ 10 8 7
♢ 9 6 2	♢ Q 6 5	♢ 9 6 3 2
♣ 8 4	♣ K J 9 8 6 5 3	♣ 8 4 3

Answers:

Bid (2 pts.)   Reason (3 pts.)

1.   3♢   This is the same 'Flint' request to partner to transfer
to 3♡ as you used in **10B.**, No. 2. When he bids 3♡
you will take out into 3♣ which you expect him to pass.

2.   3♣   Opener will take this as a request to show four-card
suits in ascending order. If you can discover a club fit,
this hand will probably run to a slam in that suit.

3.   No   Following a 2♣ opening, 2 N.T. is the only opener's
Bid   rebid which can be passed below game level.

Section 4

OPENER'S REBIDS

The Basic Rules

WHEN partner has responded to an opening bid with a limit bid, either a suit raise or no-trumps, opener's obligation to rebid is cancelled. He must now decide whether to pass, convert to what he considers a safer contract, or investigate towards a possibly better contract, either part-score, game, or even possibly slam.

If the response has been a change-of-suit which forces opener to speak again he should aim, as far as possible, at clarifying the shape and strength of his hand, though this often cannot be completed until a later round of bidding.

So, having studied the actual opening bids and the reasons for them in Section 1, let's now see how the auction gradually builds up to the final contract, each member of the partnership either denying, showing, or enquiring about values other than those already shown, if more information is still required.

1. *Following a Responder's Limit Bid:*

1♡—1NT   Responder has shown 6-9 pts. According to strength, opener may pass 1 N.T., raise to 2 N.T. on 17-18 pts. or to 3 N.T. on 19 pts. He may convert to two of his original suit (or more if strong) or show a second biddable suit which, at the two-level, would not be forcing.

1♣—1NT   Facing a 1♣ opening, 1 N.T. shows 8-10 pts., so the
2♡   above values may be reduced to allow for this.

1♠—2NT   This response has shown 10-12 pts., and again opener
3♡   may elect to pass, raise to 3 N.T., sign off in 3♠ or bid game. He can, if expedient, show a new suit which, at the three-level, is a one-round force. A 3 N.T. response shows 13-15 pts, and can obviously be passed or converted to a four-level suit contract.

1◇—3NT   If this is below game level (because in a minor) the
4◇   take-out is forcing, as it removes an existing game contract to one below game level. The 3 N.T. response is not a shut-out bid and opener may, if strong, initiate slam investigations.

1♣—2♣   This weak limit bid, showing four-card trump support
and 6-9 pts., can be passed or raised to game. Opener
1♡—2♡   may also use a Trial Bid which shows doubt as to
3♢—3♢   whether a game should be bid. It asks responder to
or 4♡   convert to the original suit at the three-level on a
minimum raise, to raise to game on a maximum or, on
an intermediate hand, to let his decision rest on the
trial-bid suit.

1♣—3♣   Following a strong limit bid at the three-level, opener
4♣   can elect to pass, bid game direct or, if a slam now
seems possible, start investigations. A new suit bid
at this stage is a cue bid, i.e. a control-showing bid,
in reply to which responder should show his own lowest-
ranking control.

2. *Following a Change-of-Suit Response:*

On a Minimum Hand:

1♠—2♢   A simple repeat of the suit opened is a sign-off rebid.
2♣ or   A rebid in a second, lower-ranking suit no higher than
2♡   the two-level shows a second biddable suit and promises
no additional values. Neither rebid is forcing.

1♢—1♡   A six-card suit should always be bid and rebid before
1♠   a four-card suit *unless* the four-card suit is a major
which can be shown at the one-level. Here, if 6-4 in
BUT   diamonds and spades, unless much better than mini-
1♢—2♣   mum, opener should rebid 2♢ if the level is raised
2♢   by a response of 2♣.

On a Better-than-Minimum Hand:

1♡—1♠   A jump rebid in the original suit is a strong though
3♡   non-forcing limit bid, showing seven playing-tricks at
that suit. It also slows a 6-card trump suit.

1♡—1♠   A raise of responder's suit shows support in addition
2♠   to the values for an opening bid. Always raise to the full
value of the hand, i.e. to the three-level or even direct
1♡—1♠   to game if strength permits. Though limit bids, these
3♠ or   last two are highly encouraging, not shut-out bids, show-
4♠   ing that opener is not willing to play at any lesser level.

On a Strong Hand:

1♡ —1♠ 3♣	A jump rebid in a new suit is unconditionally forcing to game. A new suit bid at the three-level when responder has bid at the two-level is also forcing, for which
1♡ —2◇ 3♣	reason a player with a weakish hand must be careful not to get into a situation where there is no sensible rebid other than a forcing one, a factor which may have a bearing on the choice of opening bid.

If Responder Forces:

1♡ —3♣ 3♡	On single-suited hands, make a neutral rebid in the original suit, confirming suit length or, lacking a rebiddable suit, make the minimum available rebid in
1◇ —2♡ 3 NT	no-trumps unless strong enough to make a jump rebid in no-trumps, showing a hand good enough for a 2 N.T. rebid in a non-forcing sequence.
1♡ —3♣ 3◇	With a second possible trump suit (biddable suit) take the earliest chance, i.e. at the rebid, to show it.
1♡ —3♣ 4♣	A raise of responder's suit, particularly if this by-passes the 3 N.T. level, is highly encouraging. A jump rebid in opener's original suit shows a solid and self-supporting
1♣ —2♡ 4♣	suit. (This applies at any time when a forcing situation is in being.)

3. Opener's Second Round No-Trump Limit Bids:

1♡ —1♠ 1NT	Facing a one-level response, 1 N.T. = 15-16 pts. 2 N.T. = 17+ to 18 pts. 3 N.T. = 19 pts.
1♡ —2◇	Facing a two-level response, 2 N.T. = 15-16 pts. 3 N.T. = 18+ pts.

1♡ —1♠ 2NT—3♡ ?	A return to opener's original suit after his 2 N.T. rebid is forcing, requiring him to rebid 3 N.T. or four of the suit, in the knowledge that responder has no better than three-card trump support. (A responding hand with four-card trump support, particularly for a major, would have raised the suit initially to the three-level or now made a Delayed Game Raise.)

4. "Swiss" Convention: (one variation of many)

When the opening has been 1♡ or 1♣ an immediate reponse of
4♣ or 4◇ is conventional. Both show specific holdings in a hand

which is under strength for a forcing take-out but good enough to demand at least a game contract. The raise to 4♣ shows four-card trump support, two aces, and 13-15 points, while the raise to 4◇ shows four-card trump support, three aces, and again, 13-15 points.

1♠—4◇	If opener merely repeats his suit at game level he shows
4♠	no interest in a possible slam. He may, however, bid an immediate 4 N.T. which, as he already knows the
1♡—4♣	number of aces held by responder, asks for kings on
4 NT	the 'Blackwood' scale.

5.   Replies to Responder's "Fourth Suit Forcing" Rebids:

1♡—1♠	Responder is suggesting the values for a game contract
2♣—2◇	with the accent on no-trumps. The fourth suit bid is a one-round force though it does not guarantee a
1♡—1♠	further bid when made at the two-level. With a good
2♣—2◇	stop in the fourth suit responder could himself rebid
2 NT or	in no-trumps, but as he does not do so, he is seeking
3 NT	help from opener in the suit, in which he, responder, has only a partial guard. Opener should give preference
1♡—1♠	to a rebid in no-trumps if he holds a guard or partial
2♣—2◇	guard in the fourth suit, bidding 2 N.T. or 3 N.T.
2♡ or	according to strength. Failing ability to help with the
2♠ or	fourth suit, opener must rebid as most appropriate to
3♣	describe his hand further.
1♡—1♠	A bid in the fourth suit made at the three-level promises
2◇—3♣	the ability to make at least one further bid if needed to reach the best game contract. Opener should again rebid as appropriate to his hand, giving priority to a bid of 3 N.T. if he holds the fourth suit stopped or partially stopped.

There are other more advanced sequences for use, for

1◇—1♡	instance, when responder has a genuine strong two-
2♣—2♠	suiter to show, and wants to play in one of his suits.
2NT—3♡	Here his 3♡ rebid would indicate a strong spade-heart two-suiter, asking for opener's preference.

6.   After a Strong Two Opening (2◇, 2♡, 2♠):

2♡—2NT   The Strong Two is forcing for one round with a responder's negative of 2 N.T. Any positive response makes the sequence forcing to game.

2♠—2NT   A simple opener's rebid at the three-level, either in
3♣   the original or a new suit, is non-forcing, and though
          responder's only absolute obligation is to show prefer-
2♠—2NT   ence, either by passing or 'correcting', he will raise
3◇   if he possibly can.   Therefore, if wishing to reach a
          game at all costs, opener must make either a jump to
2♡—2NT   game, a jump rebid in a new suit (forcing if below game
4◇ or   level), or a forcing "reverse". Responder is now re-
3♠   sponsible for seeing that the best game contract is
          reached.

2♡—4♡   When responder has made the ace-denial bid of a jump
4 NT   to four of opener's suit, 4 N.T. would, of course, be
          the Acol Direct King convention, bypassing the request
          for aces and asking for kings on the 'Blackwood'
          scale.

7.   After a Two Club Opening Bid:

2♣   is unconditionally forcing to game unless opener rebids
          2 N.T. Responder's negative is 2◇ and his second
          negative, if no more constructive bid is available, is
          2 N.T. Opener's no-trump rebids have already been
          covered in Section 3.

2♣—2◇   The suit rebid is unconditionally forcing to game.
2♠   Thereafter the bidding develops naturally.

2♣—2◇   A jump rebid by opener is a conventional request to
3♡   responder to show any one ace he may hold in spite of
          his 2◇ denial, by a cue-bid. With no ace he should
          rebid 3 N.T.

8.   After a Pre-Emptive Opening Three-Bid:

3♡—3♠   A change-of-suit below game level is a one-round force.
          In a major, shows a good suit and suggests game in it.

3♠—4♣   In a minor suggests a possible slam in *opener's* suit.

3◇—3NT   This is intended to play and opener should not 'rescue'
          in panic.

Section 4
OPENER'S REBIDS
Exercises

♠♡♣◇♠♡♣◇♠♡♣◇♠♡♣◇♠♡♣◇♠♡♣◇♠♡♣◇

No. 1　♠ 8 5　　　a) 1♡—3♡　b) 1♡—2 NT　c) 1♡—3◇
　　　♡ A Q 9 8 6 5　　?
　　　◇ K 8
　　　♣ J 10 6

Answers: (a) With a minimum Acol light opener you refuse partner's invitation to go to game by passing his 3♡ limit bid.

(b) The 2 N.T. limit bid, showing 10-12 pts., leaves it up to you to judge the best final contract. Simply convert to 3♡.

(c) Partner is forcing you to speak again, so make a neutral rebid of 3♡ which merely confirms heart length.

(Bids : No Bid, 3♡, and 3♡.)

No. 2　♠ K Q 9 7 3　a) 1♠—2♣　b) 1♠—2 N.T.　c)1♠—3♠
　　　♡ A Q J 8 2　　?　　　　?　　　　　?
　　　◇ 9 6 3
　　　♣ —

Answers: (a) You opened 1♠ because you had a sensible rebid if partner responded in a minor, which is just what he has done. Rebid 2♡ as you had planned.

(b) Sometimes the auction takes a course you would have preferred it not to do, as it has done here. You can't leave partner to languish in 2 N.T., even though a new suit rebid at the three-level is forcing, so bid 3♡. After all, you have excellent 'shape', and a game in either major might well be successful.

(c) Again, basing your action on 'shape', you realise that it won't take much luck to make 4♠ a successful contract, so accept the invitation and bid it.

(Bids: 2♡, 3♡, and 4♠.)

108 ACOL-ITE'S QUIZ

No. 3 ♠ Q J 7   a) 1♡—2◇   b) 1♡—2NT   c) 1♡—3♡
       ♡ A Q 9 2   ?   ?   ?
       ◇ K 7 3   (Using a 12-14 pt. no-trump you rightly
       ♣ K J 8   opened 1♡ instead of choosing a 'pre-
                    pared' 1♣.)

Answers : (a) No need, of course, for a 'prepared 'opening when
you have the strength for a sensible rebid in any situation, and
when the response is 2◇ you rebid 2 N.T. This, over a two-level
response, shows 15-16 pts.

(b) Facing 10-12 pts., which responder has announced, you
simply raise him to 3 N.T. You have no ambitions towards a slam
or a suit contract in preference to no-trumps.

(c) You could bid a direct 4♡, but there is no harm in telling
responder that you have an evenly-balanced hand which was too
strong for a 12-14 pt. no-trump opening bid. He will then judge
whether to pass 3 N.T. or 'correct' to 4♡.

(Bids : 2 N.T., 3 N.T., and 3 N.T.)

No. 4 ♠ A Q 9 6 2 a) 1♠—1 NT   b) 1♠—2♡   c) 1♠—2♣
       ♡ K Q 6   ?   ?   ?
       ◇ Q J 5
       ♣ J 6

Answers : (a) Here you have to choose between letting your
partner play in 1 N.T. or taking out into 2♠—either may be wrong.
But as partner could not support spades he may well have something in clubs. Seven tricks in no-trumps may be easier than eight
in spades, so pass.

(b) Give a simple raise to 3♡. Partner is certain to have at least
a five-card heart suit and with your club weakness you can hardly
bid no-trumps at this stage.

(c) Partner has shown a minimum of 8 pts. and a biddable club
suit—your own weakness. Rebid 2 N.T. to show 15-16 pts., and
leave it to partner to decide on further action, if any.

(Bids : No Bid, 3♡, and 2 N.T.)

No. 5   ♠ A J 8 5   a) 1♠—2♣   b) 1♠—3♠   c) 1♠—2◇
      ♡ A Q 8 4   ?   ?   2♡—3♣
      ◇ Q 10 3   ?
      ♣ Q 6

Answers :   (a) Partner has shown at least 8 pts. and a biddable club suit—your own weakest holding. Rebid 2 N.T. to show your balanced 'shape' and count, 15-16 pts. (You could not consider opening 1 N.T. as you were using 'weak'.)

(b) Never bid around the mulberry bush when you know the best final resting place. Simply go to 4♠ which you know will find four-card support and 10-12 pts. in partner's hand.

(c) Partner's 3♣ is 'fourth suit forcing' convention, not showing clubs, which he could do by rebidding in no-trumps, but asking whether you can help with a partial club stop with a view to playing in no-trumps. Confirm his hopes by rebidding 3 N.T.

                         (Bids : 2 N.T., 4♠, and 3 N.T.)

No. 6   ♠ A 6 2   a) 1♡—1♠   b) 1♡—2♠   c) 1♡—1♠
      ♡ A Q 10 8   2NT—3♠   3NT—4♡   2NT—3♡
      ◇ K J 6   ?   ?   ?
      ♣ Q J 8

Answers :   (a) You showed your full values by your original 2 N.T. rebid, in spite of which responder only wants to play in spades. Respect his decision which is made in the knowledge that you have 16+ to 18 pts., by passing.

(b) When partner makes a game force you rebid 3 N.T., not just 2 N.T., to show your 17 to 18 pts. When he next bids 4♡ your hand must be worth another try—bid 4♠ and leave it to him.

(c) Responder's 3♡, which is a return to the suit opened after the 2 N.T. rebid, is forcing, and gives opener the choice between bidding 3 N.T. or 4♡ in the knowledge that responder, lacking four-card heart support, could not bid this himself. This is a good hand for no-trump play, so rebid 3 N.T.

                    (Bids : No Bid, 4♠, and 3 N.T.)

No. 7   ♠ K J 6 2   a) 1♡—2◇   b) 1♡—1♠   c) 1♡—2 NT
       ♡ A Q J 5 3   ?   ?   ?
       ◇ Q 6
       ♣ K 5

Answers :   (a) Your hand is too good for a rebid of 2♡, and the general quality is not good enough for a 'reverse' into 2♠. After all, you're not risking very much by a count-showing rebid of 2 N.T. facing a partner who is good enough to make a change-of-suit response at the two-level.

(b) Raise direct to 4♠. There should be a play for game even if responder's hand is minimum, so you must not risk bidding only 3♠, which he might pass.

(c) Just raise quietly to 3 N.T., for which you have ample points. With at least one good honour card in all four suits, your hand must be invaluable to a partner who himself has 10-12 pts.

(Bids : 2 N.T., 4♠, and 3 N.T.)

No. 8   ♠ A Q 9 6 4   a) 1♠—2◇   b) 1♠—2♡   c) 1♠—2 NT
       ♡ 5   ?   ?   ?
       ◇ K Q J 7 3
       ♣ A J

Answers :   (a) Note first that you had no worries about whether to open 1♠ or 1◇ because clearly you were strong enough to have no rebid problems after a 1♠ bid. When partner responds 2◇, your second suit, rebid 3♣. This, being a new suit at the three-level is forcing so you ensure yourself another chance to bid and, when you've heard responder's rebid, will more than probably go 'slamming'.

(b) Rebid 3◇, your second suit, which is again forcing, though with the lack of heart fit your sights are set on the best game contract rather than a slam at this moment.

(c) Show your second suit with 3◇—forcing. This will warn responder that you are two-suited, which means a weakness in the other two suits. Leave him to judge the next move.

(Bids: 3♣, and 3◇, and 3◇.)

No. 9   ♠ A Q J 6 5   a) 1♠—1 NT   b) 1♠—2♡   c) 1♠—3 NT
        ♡ K 9   ?   ?   ?
        ◇ K Q 10 9
        ♣ A 5

Answers : (a) With 19 pts. opposite to a partner who can respond at all, even just 1 N.T., you want to be in game, and the sooner you get there without giving away the make-up of your hand, the better. Raise to 3 N.T.

(b) A whale of a hand, especially facing a partner who can respond at the two-level. Bid 3◇, forcing as it is a new suit at the three-level, on the way to the best game or possibly slam.

(c) Responder is showing 13-15 pts. You have a powerful hand which must really now produce a slam. Bid 6 N.T. direct as even if your combined total is only $32\frac{1}{2}$ pts., you have a five-card suit which adds to your strength.

(Bids : 3 N.T., 3◇, and 6 N.T.)

No. 10   ♣ A Q 10 5   a) 1♠—2♡   b) 1♠—2♣   c) 1♠—3◇
        ♡ Q J 6   ?   ?   ?
        ◇ K Q 10 7
        ♣ K 3

Answers : (a) A one-round force of 3◇ is your rebid here. This hand is certainly going at least to game, but you are not yet sure whether the best denomination will be no-trumps, hearts, or even, depending on partner's rebid, a slam somewhere.

(b) Your count here justifies a rebid of 3 N.T. when partner can respond at the two-level. Remember that a rebid of 2◇ would be a gross understatement of the hand—and might be passed anyway, as might 2 N.T.—when you want to be in game.

(c) Raise to 4◇, firmly by-passing any suggestion of a 3 N.T. contract. You are heading for a slam anyway, though more than probably partner's force in diamonds is because of a strong spade fit.

(Bids : 3◇, 3 N.T., and 4◇.)

No. 11 ♠ Q 9 2   a) 1♡—1 NT   b) 1♡—1♠   c) 1♡—2♠
       ♡ A J 10 7   ?   ?   ?
       ♢ A Q 6   (Using a 12-14 pt. no-trump you rightly
       ♣ K J 6   opened 1♡ instead of choosing a 'pre-
                         pared' 1♣.)

Answers : (a) Your hand is good enough to *invite* partner to advance to 3 N.T., by raising to 2 N.T. This shows 17-18 pts. which, if he has 8-9 pts., has every chance of yielding a game.

(b) Make a limit bid of 2 N.T., showing 17 to 18 points. This is, of course, non-forcing, though highly invitational.

(c) In (b) you were able to show your values with a bid of 2 N.T. Now, when partner has forced, he will never have any idea of your strength if you don't do better than that. Bid 3 N.T., which in this situation shows the same 17 to 18 pts.

(Bids : 2 N.T., 2 N.T., and 3 N.T.)

No. 12 ♠ A Q 10 8   a) 1♠—2♡   b) 1♠—2♣   c) 1♠—3♢
       ♡ Q J 8   3♢—4♢   3 NT—4♣   4♢—4 NT
       ♢ K Q 10 6   ?   ?   ?
       ♣ K 3

Answers : (a) This hand is almost identical with No. 10 though now the bidding is carried one round further. In this first sequence it must be clear that a slam is in the wind. Your partner will know that your forcing rebid of 3♢ may have been made on a short suit in spite of which he is raising—at the same time by-passing the 3 N.T. level. Start investigations with 4 N.T.

(b) Your partner's 4♣ rebid, which removes an existing game contract into one below game, is forcing. Clearly he has long clubs and dislikes the idea of no-trumps. Raise him to 5♣.

(c) Your partner must have a big hand because, as an Acol player, he would only force the issue of a slam with greater strength than he needed for his original game force of 3♢. Just answer his 'Blackwood' question as to how many aces you hold by bidding 5♢ to show one.

(Bids : 4 N.T., 5♣, and 5♢.)

No. 13 ♠ A Q J 6   a) 1◇—2♣ b) 1◇—1♡ c) 1◇—1 NT
      ♡ 7   ?   ?   ?
      ◇ A J 10 7 5 3
      ♣ 8 2

Answers: (a) This hand is not strong enough for anything but a simple rebid in diamonds at the two-level. If you rebid 2♠ you would be showing strength you don't possess by 'reversing'.

(b) You should always bid and *rebid* a six-card suit unless holding a four-card major suit which can be shown at the one-level. Here just this situation exists, so take you opportunity to rebid 1♠.

(c) You would be very ill-advised to do anything except take out into 2◇. Partner would surely have taken his opportunity to show a four-card spade suit at the one-level if he had it, so no spade fit has been missed and this is not a hand for a no-trump contract.

(Bids : 2◇, 1♠, and 2◇.)

No. 14 ♠ A Q 10 9   a) 1♡—1♠ b) 1♡—2◇ c) 1♡—3♡
      ♡ A Q J 8 5   ?   ?   ?
      ◇ K 7 5
      ♣ 8

Answers: (a) The last thing you really expected was that partner would respond 1♠! However, even if his hand is completely minimum for this you feel there must be a good play for game. Bid 4♠ direct which is not a shut-out bid, because responder will realise that you were not willing to risk playing below game-level.

(b) 'Reverse' into 2♠. This is a one-round force and responder will know that your hearts, because you bid them first, are longer than your spades, and that your hand is strong enough to be given preference to hearts at the three-level.

(c) Distributionally there may well be a slam on here. Try it out with a cue-bid of 3♠ which, in this context, shows first-round control of spades, not necessarily a suit. It is, of course, forcing.

(Bids : 4♠, 2♠, and 3♠.)

No. 15 ♠ K 8 7 2   a) 1♡—2♣ b) 1♡—1♠ c) 1♡—3♣
     ♡ A K Q J 10 4   ?   ?   ?
     ◇ 7
     ♣ A 9

Answers : (a) A jump rebid of 3♡ will tell partner that you have seven playing tricks at hearts—just short of an opening Strong Two. This is a very strong limit bid, though not forcing, and a responder who could bid at the two-level is unlikely to pass.

(b) Raise direct to 4♠, not, as we have already seen, a shut-out bid, but showing that partner's response has hit the jackpot and that you are not willing to play below game level. If responder himself is strong, he will take the hint and go slamming.

(c) When a forcing situation is in being, as it is here, a jump rebid shows a solid and self-supporting trump suit. Rebid 4♡, not as a stop bid but to encourage responder, who need not now worry about having possibly little or no heart fit.

(Bids : 3♡, 4♠, and 4♡.)

No. 16 ♠ A Q   a) 1♡—2♡ b) 1♡—3♡ c) 1♡—3♣
     ♡ A 10 9 6 4 2   ?   ?   ?
     ◇ 9 5 4
     ♣ K J

Answers : (a) You are very doubtful about going to game facing a mere 2♡ raise. On the other hand your 'shape' is good and it won't take much to produce a game if responder's bits and pieces are in the right place—which particularly applies to diamonds. Ask him by making a trial bid of 3◇—the suit you are worried about. You will meet partner's responses in the next section.

(b) This time you have no hesitation about going to 4♡. Note, by the way, that a rebid in diamonds now would be a cue-bid, not a trial bid.

(c) Rebid your hearts at the simple three-level, showing a rebiddable suit and no other biddable suit. A neutral bid.

(Bids : 3◇, 4♡, and 3♡.)

No. 17 ♠ A Q 3   a) 1♡ —1♠ b) 1♡ —1 NT c) 1♡ —2◇
       ♡ K J 7 3   ?   ?   ?
       ◇ J 9 2
       ♣ A 8 7   (Using a 12-14 pt. no trump, you opened
                    one of your 4-card suit)

Answers: (a) Rebid 1 N.T., showing 15-16 pts., in a hand just too strong to open 1 N.T.

(b) Partner has shown 6-9 points in a hand unable to support hearts. Just pass.

(c) On this somewhat flat hand be content with a simple rebid of 2 N.T., showing 15-16 points. Await developments, if any.

(Bids: 1 N.T., No Bid, and 2 N.T.)

No. 18 ♠ A J 10 7   a) 1♡—1 NT   b) 1♡—1♠   c) 1♡—2♣
       ♡ A Q 7 2   ?   ?   ?
       ◇ K J 6
       ♣ A 5   (You opened 1♡ instead of 1♠ because
                    this hand is very suitable for play in no-
                    trumps *unless* responder raises hearts or
                    himself bids spades.)

Answers: (a) A rare type of hand, this, on which you want to make it easy for responder to raise hearts or show a spade suit. When he does neither you are sure a major suit fit is missing and raise him to 3 N.T. for which you have the values.

(b) This time responder comes up with a biddable spade suit. There might now be a slam on—test the market with a forcing 3♣ which responder will know may be on a short suit. Anyway, see what he bids next—you can always put him back into spades later.

(c) As responder has neither raised hearts nor bid spades, show your values by a jump to 3 N.T., the denomination you always fancied for this hand.

(Bids: 3 N.T., 3♣, 3 N.T.)

No. 19 ♠ A Q 10 8 6 5   a) 1♠—3♠   b) 1♠—4♣   c) 1♠—2♡
      ♡ K Q 4   ?   ?   ?
      ◇ K 6
      ♣ A 3

Answers: (a) With this strong hand facing a 3♠ raise you must start thinking in terms of a possible slam. But go a little warily before committing yourself to a contract higher than 4♠—investigate where partner's goodies lie by a cue bid of 4♣, to which he will reply by showing his lowest-ranking first-round control.

(b) Partner has made a 'Swiss' conventional response showing trump agreement, two aces, and 13-15 points. Bid 4 N.T. asking for kings on the 'Blackwood' scale—you've already been told about his aces, and want to be sure that, missing one ace between you, partner has the ♠K.

(c) As soon as partner mentions hearts, a guaranteed 5-card suit, you start thinking of higher things. But you need more information. Bid 3♠ (a 'high reverse') showing a 16+ pt. hand and asking partner to clarify his own hand.

                               (Bids: 4♣, 4 N.T., and 3♠.)

No. 20 ♠ 10   a) 1♡—2♡   b) 1♡—2♣   c) 1♡—4◇
      ♡ K Q J 10 8 6   ?   ?   ?
      ◇ A K 2
      ♣ 7 5 3

Answers: (a) You could bid 4♡ and then find partner with a flat hand except for the ♠K and ♡A—x—x—x, in which case you might well go two down. If, however, he can help with either honours or a shortage in clubs, 4♡ becomes a good proposition. Ask him with a trial bid of 3♣.

(b) Show seven playing tricks with a 6-card heart suit by a jump rebid of 3♡. Partner will understand that you would like to be in game but that, for your money, this should be in hearts.

(c) Simply sign off in 4♡ saying that, in spite of your knowledge of what partner is showing by his 'Swiss' 4◇, you have no wish to reach a slam contract. After all, he has not got the values for a forcing bid.

                               (Bids: 3♣, 3♡, and 4♡.)

No. 21 ♠ 7   a) 2♡—2 NT   b) 2♡—2♠ c) 2♡—3♡
       ♡ A Q J 10 8 5   ?   ?   ?
       ◇ A Q J 10 3
       ♣ 4

Answers : (a) Show your second suit, diamonds, at the lowest available level. Knowing that you have a strong two-suiter responder will try to help you into a game in the one he likes best, though he is not forced to bid again. If he gives you preference to 3♡ it would be worth trying 4♡.

(b) The 2♠ 'positive' response makes the sequence forcing to game. No need to hurry—just show your two-suiter by a rebid of 3◇.

(c) This 'positive' response shows trump support and at least one ace or void. Bid 4◇ showing the cheapest first-round control, not necessarily a suit now that hearts are agreed, and await responder's rebid.

(Bids : 3◇, 3◇, and 4◇.)

No. 22
       ♠ 7   a) 2♡—2 NT   b) 2♡—3♡   c) 2♡—3 NT
       ♡ A Q J 10 8 7   ?   ?   ?
       ◇ A K J 9 7 5
       ♣ —

Answers : (a) You want to be in game in one of your red suits despite partner's negative response, so you must force him to speak again to tell you which of them he prefers. Rebid 4◇ and he must either 'correct' to 4♡ or raise to 5◇.

(b) Be a bit clever here—you greatly want to know if partner has the ♠A (a void is extremely unlikely on your hand). Cue-bid 4♣, your lower-ranking control. If partner has the ♣A he will know at least that this is duplication of values. If he bids 4◇, it will be showing a void, but if he bids 4♠ you can now investigate for the grand slam contract.

(c) Partner has 10-11 pts. but no biddable suit. 6♡ is not likely to depend on worse than a heart finesse, so bid it.

(Bids : 4◇, 4♣, and 6♡.)

No. 23

♠ A K Q 9 4   a) 2♡—3♡   b) 2♡—2NT   c) 2♡—3 NT
♡ A K J 8 7 3   ?   ?   ?
◇ 4
♣ 6

Answers :   (a) Partner's 3♡ is, of course, showing heart agreement and at least one ace or void. You can feel confident of no heart losers, spades should take care of themselves, so whether you go to a little or grand slam depends on whether he has one or two aces (he *might* have none and a spade void !) Bid 4 N.T. to find out.

(b) You certainly want to be in a game, either in hearts or spades, so 'reverse' into 3♠, which is forcing for one round. Partner must raise to 4♠ or 'correct' to 4♡, whichever he thinks best in the knowledge that your hearts are the longer.

(c) Partner has 10-11 points so a slam might be on the map. But, from your point of view, 3 N.T. is not a good idea. Rebid into 4♠ to see if partner has a fit for this suit.

(Bids : 4 N.T., 3♠, and 4♠.)

No. 24

♠ A K J 10 6 5 3   a) 2♠—2 NT   b) 2♠—3♠   c) 2♠—3 NT
♡ K 7   ?   ?   ?
◇ 9
♣ K Q 6

Answers :   (a) With what is really only a minimum for the original 2♠ opening, simply rebid 3♠. Partner is under no obligation to bid again but, knowing how good your hand is, he may be able to put you to game when he would have passed a lesser opening bid.

(b) Partner has at least one ace or void, but he will have to make any slam try there is to be. Bid 4♠ and leave it to him to pass or bid on once he knows you have no extra values to show.

(c) This time partner has 10-11 pts. Simply convert to 4♠ knowing that you probably have at least three aces to lose—partner must have some diamond honours and possibly the ♡Q.

(Bids : 3♠, 4♠, and 4♠.)

No. 25

♠ K 6 4   a) 2♡—2 NT   b) 2♡—3♡   c) 2♡—4♣
♡ A K Q 10 8 7 4   ?   ?   ?
♢ A 3
♣ 8

Answers :   (a) Just quietly rebid 3♡ and hope that responder,
knowing you have at least eight playing tricks, will be able to put
you to game.

(b) Responder has at least one ace or void, not necessarily
only one ace or void, and a trump fit. It cannot do any harm to cue-
bid your lowest (only) other control by bidding 4♢. If responder
can show the ♠A there should be a good play for 6♡.

(c) As 2♡ is a forcing bid, a forcing situation is in being, so
responder's 4♣ shows a long solid self-supporting club suit. Knowing he needs no support for this—and that you will be able to use
it for discards if you won't allow him to play in clubs, get on with
finding out if he has the ♠A too by bidding 4 N.T.

(Bids : 3♡, 4♢, and 4 N.T.)

No. 26

♠ A 10 9 6 5 3   a) 2♠—2 NT   b) 2♠—3♢   c) 2♠—3 NT
♡ A K J 8 7   ?   ?   ?
♢ A Q
♣ —

Answers :   (a) In spite of the strength of your hand you don't
really want to be in game if partner has a Yarborough. Bid 3♡
showing your second suit. If he can possibly do so, partner will bid
again, possibly to put you to 4♡ or 4♠, or just to 'correct' to 3♠.

(b) Responder can make a positive bid without the ace and
queen of his suit, which he would not do if he had spade support
to show at this stage—far more likely to be helpful than 3♢. The
sequence is now forcing to game, so show your second suit—you
can always put the contract back into diamonds.

(c) Here, not much caring for a no-trump contract, you can show
your hearts over 3 N.T., leaving it to partner to choose between
4♡ and 4♠.

(Bids : 3♡, 3♡, and 4♡.)

No. 27

♠ K Q   a) 2♣—2◇   b) 2♣—2 NT   c) 2♣—2 NT
♡ A K Q 7 5   ?   ?   3♡—4♡
◇ A K 9   ?
♣ A 6 3

Answers : (a) A simple bid of 2♡, showing the best suit, makes the sequence forcing to game. At this stage responder will not know whether you have more than one suit, but that will develop later.

(b) 2 N.T. is positive, though it should not include an ace. For the moment simply show your heart suit and await developments.

(c) It is to be hoped that you did not notice the rebid in (c) before you had answered (b), as this is only a continuation of the same sequence. With the 2 N.T. showing 'positve' values, and now finding a heart fit, the least you can do is investigate further with 4 N.T. If responder has not got the ♠A he will surely have club honours to make 6♡ worth bidding.

(Bids : 2♡, 3♡, and 4 N.T.)

No. 28

♠ A K Q J 10 6 2   a) 2♣—2◇   b) 2♣—2♡   c) 2♣—2◇
♡ K Q 7   ?   ?   3♠—4◇
◇ K Q   ?
♣ A

Answers : (a) If partner has just one red ace and nothing else, it would not give him a positive response to 2♣. A jump rebid by opener in this sequence now asks him to cue-bid it if he has one and, if not, to rebid 3 N.T. So rebid 3♠ and, if he bids 3 N.T. to show no ace, convert to 4♠.

(b) Jump-rebid 3♠ to ask partner to cue-bid any ace he may hold —very hopeful now that he has given a positive response. If he has none, the worst that can happen is that you will play in 4♠, but he's got to have enough points to make up a positive, so will surely have one ace.

(c) This is a continuation of the sequence in (a). Partner has the ◇A which makes 6♠ the obvious contract.

(Bids: 3♠, 3♠, and 6♠.)

No. 29

♠ A K Q J 10 6 5 2   First, what's the right opening bid here?
♡ —   Got it? Then:
♢ 6   a) 4 NT—5♣   b) 4 NT—5♡   c) 4 NT—5♢
♣ A K Q J   ?   ?   ?

Answers : (a) Note the vital importance of discovering which ace, if any, responder holds. 5♣ denies any ace, so just convert to 6♠, the contract you expect to make.

(b) Here responder holds the useless ♡A, so again just convert to 6♠. Note that responder must never disturb opener's rebid, whether this is at the five-level or higher.

(c) Now responder has the vital ♢A, and nothing but a first-round ruff could defeat 7♠, so bid it.

(Bids : 6♠, 6♠, and 7♠.)

No. 30

♠ A 7   a) 2♣—2♢   b) 2♣—2♠   c) 2♣—4♣
♡ A K 3   ?   ?   ?
♢ A K Q J 6 5 4
♣ 5

Answers : (a) 2♢ is, of course, a negative response, so 3♢ is showing your suit, not raising responder's !

(b) A positive response with a biddable spade suit—not that you particularly want to play this in spades, but a diamond slam is a near certainty so get on with investigations via 4 N.T.

(c) Partner has a solid and self-supporting club suit, needing no help from you. If you are declarer you will be able to use it for discards of your losers, and if he is declarer your diamonds will serve the same purpose for him. So take your pick as long as you bid the grand slam, 7♣ or 7♢ or, if you are playing M.P. Pairs, you will want to go for 7 N.T.

(Bids : 3♢, 4 N.T., either 7♣, 7♢, or 7 N.T.)

Section 4

OPENER'S REBIDS
Competition Quiz

♠♡♣◇♠♡♣◇♠♡♣◇♠♡♣◇♠♡♣◇♠♡♣◇♠♡♣◇

IN competition against another player, each in turn should answer a full page of six questions. As an added exercise, you might like to decide on the correct opening bid on each hand before going on to the scoring questions on rebids. You met the opening bids in Section I, but note that no hand in this section is to be opened with a bid in no-trumps, from which you must assume that your agreed no-trump range is either too weak or too strong.

1A.

1. ♠ 9 3
   ♡ K J 8 5
   ◇ A Q 10 7 4 2
   ♣ 8

   1◇—1♠
   ?

2. ♠ 9 3
   ♡ K J 10 7 2
   ◇ A K J 6 5
   ♣ 8

   1♡—1♠
   ?

3. ♠ A Q 7 5
   ♡ 8
   ◇ K Q 6 3
   ♣ K J 8 5

   1◇—1♡
   ?

Answers:
Bid (2 pts.)   Reason (3 pts.)

1. 2◇   A simple rebid in your six-card suit, which was really your only excuse for opening.

2. 2◇   With two adjacent suits you rightly opened one of the higher-ranking, leaving yourself a sensible rebid in the other.

3. 1♠   You opened one of the suit below the singleton to give yourself a sensible rebid in any circumstances.

   What would you bid next on the same hands in these sequences?

4. 1◇—1♠
   2◇—2♡
   ?

5. 1♡—2 NT
   ?

6. 1◇—1♡
   1♠—2 NT
   ?

Answers:
Bid (2 pts.)   Reason (3 pts.)

4. 3♡   When partner hits the jackpot with his second try, your 'shape' and trump fit make it worth the single raise.

5. 3◇   You can hardly leave partner languishing in 2 N.T. Even though your new suit bid at the three-level is a one-round force, show it.

6. 3 N.T.   Never mind your singleton—this is in partner's suit. Your combined values should be at least 26 pts.

1B.

1.	2.	3.
♠ A Q 7 5	♠ 5	♠ A Q J 7 2
♡ K J 10 8	♡ 7 5 4 2	♡ A 10 9 4
◇ K Q 7 6	◇ A K 6 3	◇ K 3
♣ 7	♣ A Q J 4	♣ 7 5
1♡—1♠	1◇—2♣	1♠—2◇
?	?	?

Answers:

Bid (2 pts.)   Reason (3 pts.)

1. **3♠**   You opened 1♡ to facilitate finding a possible spade fit. Counting distribution your hand, if played in this suit, is now worth 17 pts., and you can raise to the three-level.

2. **3♣**   You opened 1◇, treating the hand as a minor two-suiter. A raise to 3♣, giving partner another chance, is enough.

3. **2♡**   With a weakish hand of 5-4 shape, open one of the five-card suit and, as long as you can do so at the two-level, rebid in your four-card suit, provided it is lower in rank than your original suit.

What would you bid next on the same hands in these sequences?

4. 1♡—2♣	5. 1◇—1♠	6. 1♠—2♡
2◇—2♡	2♣—2 NT	3♡—3♠
?	?	?

Answers:

Bid (2 pts.)   Reason (3 pts.)

4. **No Bid** It sounds as if responder's hand were minimum, as all he can do is give simple preference to hearts. Pass, and be happy to make a plus-score.

5. **3 N.T.** Partner is making another try, showing 10-12 pts. as well as the biddable spade suit. This should make 3 N.T. a good proposition, even if your hearts are not very good. Partner has shown a guard in this suit, which may even make your ♡ 7 valuable!

6. **4♡**   It's anybody's guess whether 4♡ or 4♠ will be safer on this hand, but you have a certain 5-4 heart fit, and certainly no better than 5-3 in spades.

2A.

1. ♠ A 7 5
   ♡ K 8 4 2
   ◇ Q 9 3
   ♣ A 8 4

   1♣—1♠
   ?

2. ♠ A J 10 3
   ♡ K J 10 7
   ◇ A 6 4
   ♣ A J

   1♡—2♣
   ?

3. ♠ A Q 9 3
   ♡ K 8 4
   ◇ A J 8 6
   ♣ 7 2

   1♠—2♣
   ?

Answers:

Bid (2 pts.)   Reason (3 pts.)

1. 1 N.T. You opened a 'prepared' 1♣, not being strong enough for the 15-17 pt. no-trump you are using. Make your rebid in no-trumps to make it clear to partner that you are not bidding on a long club suit.

2. 3 N.T. You opened 1♡ to make it easy for partner to show a spade suit if he had one. Rebid 3 N.T., clearly the best denomination and what your hand is worth.

3. 2◇ You opened 1♠ to facilitate your rebid, which it has done. Let the auction develop quietly on this modest hand by showing your second biddable suit.

What would you bid next on the same hands in these sequences?

4. 1♣—1♡
   2♡—2 NT
   ?

5. 1♡—1♠
   ?

6. 1♠—2♡
   3♡—3 NT
   ?

Answers:

Bid (2 pts.)   Reason (3 pts.)

4. 3 N.T. When responder bid 1♡, your four-card suit, it would have been senseless to rebid 1 N.T., as you did in No. 1 above. Now he is making another try, actually in the denomination you had in mind in the first place. Raise to 3 N.T.

5. 4♠ Partner's 1♠ may have been minimum, but never leave to him what you can do yourself. A spade game contract must be worth trying.

6. No Bid Don't disturb what looks like a perfectly good contract. Partner was not forced to speak again over your 3♡, so he must have extra values to what he needed for his 2♡ bid.

2B.

1.	2.	3.
♠ A 10 9 6	♠ 8 5	♠ K Q 6
♡ 7 3	♡ A 10 9 7	♡ K J 5 4
◇ A Q 9 5	◇ K J 5	◇ A 6 2
♣ K J 4	♣ A Q 5 2	♣ K 9 5
1◇—1♡	1♡—1♠	1♡—2♣
?	?	?

Answers:

Bid (2 pts.)   Reason (3 pts.)

1. **1♠**   Take it easy—if responder can't bid a second time you don't want to be in a high contract. It would be a matter of style rather than totally wrong to rebid 1 N.T., so you may score one point for that rebid.

2. **1 N.T.**   Your second suit being a minor, it is much less urgent to show it than when it was a major.

3. **2 N.T.**   The 1♡ opening on this 16 pt. hand left you with no rebid problem. Now show your count and even distribution with a 2 N.T. rebid.

What would you bid next on the same hands in these sequences?

4. 1◇—1♡	5. 1♡—2♠	6. 1♡—2♣
1♠—2♣	?	2NT—3♡
?		?

Answers:

Bid (2 pts.)   Reason (3 pts.)

4. **2 N.T.**   Partner's 2♣ is a 'fourth suit forcing' request, not showing a club suit, but asking whether you can help to stop clubs for a no-trump contract. You can, especially as he will have a little something in clubs himself. Respond in no-trumps according to your values if you have the help he needs—in this case with a modest 14 pts., bid 2 N.T.

5. **3♣**   Although you rebid 1 N.T. when partner responded 1♠, when he forces you should take this opportunity to show any possible alternative trump suit.

6. **3 N.T.**   The 3♡ rebid, a return to your original suit after your 2 N.T. rebid, is forcing, and asks for your choice between 3 N.T. and 4♡. Partner has only three hearts, or he would have made a 3♡ limit bid in the first place or bid 4♡ now.

3A.

1. ♠ Q 9	2. ♠ J 6	3. ♠ Q 8
♡ A K 7 4 3	♡ A K Q 8 4	♡ A Q J 7 5 4
◇ K 8 5	◇ K J 5	◇ K 5
♣ Q J 6	♣ A 10 8	♣ 10 9 8
1♡—1♠	1♡—2◇	1♡—1♠
?	?	?

Answers:

Bid (2 pts.)   Reason (3 pts.)

1. 1 N.T.   With 15-16 pts. and a stop in both unbid suits, 1 N.T. is a more constructive rebid than an apparent sign-off into 2♡.

2. 3♣   This is a one-round force (a new suit at the three level) designed to get partner to clarify his hand. ♠J-x is not enough for a rebid in no-trumps and 3◇ might be passed when either 3 N.T., 4♡ or 5◇ can be made.

3. 2♡   Simply sign off in your own six-card suit. The hand has no future unless partner can bid again.

What would you bid next on the same hands in these sequences?

4. 1♡—2 NT	5. 1♡—1♠	6. 1♡—2 NT
?	?	?

Answers:

Bid (2 pts.)   Reason (3 pts.)

4. 3 N.T.   Facing 11-12 pts. you must have ample values for game. Any contract can come adrift on the rocks of a misfit, but this is clearly your best resting-place.

5. 3 N.T.   With 17-18 pts., technically your rebid is 2 N.T., but you must take your excellent heart suit into account.

6. 4♡   3 N.T. is not an attractive idea on this hand so your choice is between signing off in 3♡ or going for game. If partner's 10-12 pts. are in the right place, 4♡ should have a good chance of success.

3B. 1. ♠ A K J 6 4   2. ♠ K Q 6 3   3. ♠ A J 10 8 6 4
           ♡ 7 6   ♡ A J 10 8 6   ♡ 9 2
           ◇ J 10 8 3   ◇ K 6   ◇ A K Q 5
           ♣ A J   ♣ A 5   ♣ A

         1♣—2♡   1♡—2◇   2♠—2 NT
         ?   ?   ?

Answers:
Bid (2 pts.)   Reason (3 pts.)

1. 2 N.T.   With 14 pts. your choice is between an underbid of 2♠
            and 2 N.T., which requires 15 pts. You actually have
            14½ *and* a good five-card suit, which is adequate com-
            pensation.

2. 2♠   This 'reverse' is a one-round force showing a strong
            hand with longer hearts than spades. Partner will bid
            at least once more, if only to put you back to 3♡, but
            he will think in terms of bidding no-trumps if he has
            something in clubs.

3. 3♠   The hand was too good for a simple 1♠ opening, but
            was somewhat minimum for 2♠. Just rebid your long
            suit at the lowest available level.

         What would you bid next on the same hands in these
         sequences?

         4. 1♠—2◇   5. 1♡—2◇   6. 2♠—3♠
            3◇—3♠   2♠—3♡   ?
            ?   ?

Answers:
Bid (2 pts.)   Reason (3 pts.)

4. 4♠   By his 3♠ rebid partner is showing that, lacking the
            four-card spade support needed for an immediate 3♠
            limit bid, he thinks his hand worth another try. He
            probably has ♠Q-x-x and, with your diamond fit, this
            makes the game contract worth bidding.

5. 4♡   Partner is showing simple preference for hearts and
            lack of a club stop in reply to your forcing 2♣ reverse.
            Even so, it should be worth bidding the game, as he has
            already shown at least 8 pts.

6. 4♣   Partner has shown a trump fit and at least one ace *or*
            void. If this is in hearts he will show it in reply to your
            cue bid, after which 6♠ becomes an excellent pro-
            position.

4A.

1. ♠ A Q J 3	2. ♠ K J 9	3. ♠ A J 10 8 5 4
♡ A K Q 6 2	♡ Q J 5	♡ 8 5 2
◊ Q 4	◊ A Q 10 6	◊ K J
♣ 7 5	♣ A 8 4	♣ A Q

1♡—2♣	1◊—1♠	1♠—2♠
?	?	?

Answers:

Bid (2 pts.)   Reason (3 pts.)

1. 2♠ Strong enough to open 1♡ and 'reverse' into 2♠, a one-round force. This gives information as well as asking partner to clarify his own hand further.

2. 2 N.T. This, of course, shows a reasonably balanced hand with 17-18 pts., leaving partner to judge the best final contract.

3. 3♡ This is a Trial Bid—a one-round force—telling partner that in view of his weak response you are doubtful about bidding 4♠ direct. It also asks if he can give any 'help' in hearts, your own weak spot.

What would you bid next on the same hands in these sequences?

4. 1♡—2♣	5. 1◊—2♣	6. 1♠—2♠
2♠—2NT	?	3♡—3♠
?		?

Answers:

Bid (2 pts.)   Reason (3 pts.)

4. 3 N.T. When asked to clarify his hand, partner has neither supported spades, given preference to hearts, nor rebid clubs. He is showing a stop in diamonds, so 3 N.T. becomes a reasonable proposition.

5. 3 N.T. When partner can respond at the two-level, showing at least 8 pts., you are too good to bid a mere 2 N.T., showing a maximum of 16 pts. which might be passed out.

6. No Bid Partner is either completely minimum for his 2♠ raise or has no help for you in hearts. Be content where you are.

4B.   1. ♠ K Q J 10 7 2   2. ♠ A Q 9 8 6   3. ♠ A 9 3
      ♡ A K 7   ♡ A Q J 8 4 3   ♡ 4
      ◇ 9   ◇ 7 4   ◇ A J 5
      ♣ K 5 2   ♣ —   ♣ K Q J 10 6 5

      1♠—2◇   1♡—2♣   1♣—2♣
      ?   ?   ?

Answers:
Bid (2 pts.)   Reason (3 pts.)

1. 3♠   This jump rebid shows that you are only a trick short of
a Strong Two bid, i.e. that you have seven playing tricks
at spades, with at least a six-card spade suit.

2. 2♠   You may be low in honour points for a forcing 'reverse' but the 'shape' is magnificent, and the hand is
only a little short of a Strong Two opening.

3. 2◇   5♣ is a long way to go if 3 N.T. can be made and there
is a good chance that partner has the ♣A in his humble
response. 2◇ is a minor suit trial bid, different from a
trial bid when there has been a major suit opening.
Now you *show* a stop and ask responder if he can show
one in return.

What would you bid next on the same hands in these
sequences?

      4. 1♠—2♠   5. 1♡—2♣   6. 1♣—2♣
         ?   2♠—3♣   2◇—2♡
                 ?   ?

Answers:
Bid (2 pts.)   Reason (3 pts.)

4. 4♠   Never bid around the mulberry bush when you know
where you are going. No need for anything but a
direct 4♠ here, as even if partner can only raise to 2♠
you want to be in game.

5. 3♠   Having opened 1♡, when you bid *and rebid* spades,
partner will know that this suit, being rebiddable, is at
least a five-card suit and that, therefore, your hand is
at least 6-5 in hearts and spades—in that order.

6. 3 N.T.   Relying on your clubs and on your partner to provide
a stop in hearts, go for the no-trump game. He can
always take out if he thinks it wisest.

5A.

1. ♠ A Q J 5 3	2. ♠ K Q J 7 5 2	3. ♠ A Q J 8 6 3
♡ 7 2	♡ 6	♡ A K 10 7 4
◊ 9	◊ —	◊ 10 6
♣ A Q J 8 4	♣ K Q 9 8 7 3	♣ —
1♣—1 NT	1♣—1♡	2♠—2 NT
?	?	?

Answers:

Bid (2 pts.)   Reason (3 pts.)

1. 2♠   You can't leave partner languishing in 1 N.T.! As his hand is limited by his 1 N.T. response, your spade rebid is not a forcing reverse, and he may pass if he thinks this wisest.

2. 1♠   Yes, you open 1♣ on two equal lengthed black suits whether they are four, five or six cards long! When you rebid in spades partner will know that your clubs are at least as long, if not longer than your spades. If he can't bid again voluntarily you don't want to be in a high contract.

3. 3♡   Just that much stronger than **4B**, No. 2. Make a simple rebid in your second suit—not forcing.

What would you bid next on the same hands in these sequences?

4. 1♣—1 NT	5. 1♣—1♡	6. 2♠—2 NT
2♠—3♣	1♠—2◊	3♡—4♡
?	?	?

Answers:

Bid (2 pts.)   Reason (3 pts.)

4. 4♠   Partner's 1 N.T. has shown 8-10 pts., and now that he knows you have a black two-suiter he is encouraging you when he need not do so. In spite of your low count, bid 4♠ on 'shape'.

5. 3♠   Partner's 'fourth-suit-forcing' 2◊ is exploring for a no-trump contract (the last thing you want), from which you can safely infer that his responding hand is not minimum. Your jump bid in spades will indicate your 'shape' and will make it clear that your hand is almost completely black.

6. No Bid   Partner's original 2 N.T. makes any thought of a slam a poor idea. Pass, and be happy to have discovered a trump fit.

5B. 1. ♠ A K J 8 5 2 2. ♠ 7 3. ♠ A J 9 7 5
　　　　♡ A Q 10 9 8 7　♡ A K J 10 3　♡ K J 9 7 5 4
　　　　◇ 8　　　　　◇ A K J 7 6 2　◇ J 6
　　　　♣ —　　　　　♣ 5　　　　　♣ —

　　　　2♠—2 NT　　　2◇—2 NT　　　1♠—2♣
　　　　?　　　　　　?　　　　　　?

Answers:
Bid (2 pts.)　　　　　　　　Reason (3 pts.)

1. 4♡　You want to be in game at all costs and a simple rebid
　　of 3♡ would not be forcing. Partner's only obligation
　　now is to decide which suit you should play in, by
　　passing 4♡ or 'correcting' to 4♠.

2. 3♡　This 'reverse' is forcing so there's no need to jump.
　　Partner must raise to 4♡ or 'correct' to 4◇, showing
　　his preference. He might even be able to show real
　　diamond preference with 5◇.

3. 2♡　This hand is the odd man out, not strong enough for a
　　two-bid and not even strong enough for an opening 1♡
　　with a reverse into spades. It is an example of an
　　exception to the rule that you should bid the longer suit
　　first, but all you risk is getting preference to spades
　　which you don't really prefer!

What would you bid next on the same hands in these
sequences?

　　　4. 2♠—4♠　　　5. 2◇—4◇　　　6. 1♠—2♣
　　　　?　　　　　　?　　　　　　2♡—3♣
　　　　　　　　　　　　　　　　?

Answers:
Bid (2 pts.)　　　　　　　　Reason (3 pts.)

4. 5◇　This is a canny bid. You are now interested specific-
　　ally in the ♡K, and partner already knows *you* know
　　he has no aces. Cue-bid 5◇ and, with the ♡K, he will
　　cue-bid it in reply. He won't push you into the slam
　　by cue-bidding the ♣K if he has that and not the ♡K.

5. 5◇　As partner has announced no first round controls, no
　　thoughts of a slam arise.

6. No Bid　You've said your little all—if partner is solely club-
　　minded, the lower the contract stays, the better!

6A.

1. ♠ A Q 9 7 3	2. ♠ A 6	3. ♠ A Q J 2
♡ K Q 6	♡ A K Q J 7 4	♡ A K Q J 10 9
◇ 8 7 2	◇ K 6	◇ A 7
♣ K 5	♣ A Q 3	♣ A
1♠—4♣	2♣—2◇	2♣—2♠
?	?	?

Answers:

Bid (2 pts.) Reason (3 pts.)

1. 4♠ Partner's 4♣ was 'Swiss', showing two aces, good trump support, and 13-15 points. Even if he has 15 points, you are under strength for a slam, so just convert to 4♠.

2. 2♡ A simple rebid in your best suit, which is forcing to game.

3. 5 N.T. If partner has the values for a positive response all you need is to be sure they aren't all in the minor suits—for the Grand Slam he must have the ♠K. 5 N.T. is a Grand Slam Force in reply to which, with none of the top three spade honours he must rebid 6♣ (which you would convert to 6♠) and with one, which can only be the king, he must bid six of the agreed trump suit, which you would raise to seven. Note that you are willing to give up your hearts to play in spades.

What would you bid next on the same hands in these sequences?

4. 1♠—4♣	5. 2♣—2◇	6. 2♣—2◇
4◇*—4♠	2♡—2 NT	2♡—4◇
?	?	?
* A cue bid.		

Answers:

Bid (2 pts.) Reason (3 pts.)

4. No Bid Partner's rebid of 4♠ suit shows that he has nothing extra to show. Be content with the game contract.

5. 4♡ Give up and settle for the game contract—partner has made not only one, but two negative bids.

6. 7♡ 4◇ shows a long solid and self-supporting diamond suit missing the ace. Your hearts are so self-supporting that you can afford to play in this suit knowing that all your losers will go away on his diamonds. Bid 7 ♡ at Rubber Bridge & 7 N.T. at Duplicate.

6B.   1. ♠ A Q 9 7 3   2. ♠ A 6   3. ♠ A Q 7
        ♡ K Q 6   ♡ K 6   ♡ A K Q 10 8 6
        ◊ A 7 2   ◊ A Q 3   ◊ A 7 2
        ♣ K 5   ♣ A K Q J 7 4   ♣ A

        1♠—4♣   2♣—2◊   2♠—2◊
        ?   ?   ?

Answers:
Bid (2 pts.)   Reason (3 pts.)

1. 4 N.T.   By now you know what partner's 'Swiss' 4♣ means.
          For a successful slam it is vital to know whether he
          also has a king. Bid 4 N.T. which, as he has already
          said that he holds two aces, asks for kings on the
          'Blackwood' scale.

2. 3 N.T.   Conventionally this shows an evenly-balanced hand of
          24 or more points, but a 3♣ rebid risks the second
          negative of 3 N.T. coming from partner which might be
          disastrous. 3 N.T. from your hand, with the lead
          coming up to you, is an odds-on bet.

3. 2♡   The simple rebid in your own suit, forcing to game.

What would you bid next on the same hands in these
sequences?

        4. 1♠—4♣   5. 2♣—2♡   6. 2♣—2◊
          4◊—4♠   ?   2♡—4◊
          ?   ?

Answers:
Bid (2 pts.)   Reason (3 pts.)

4. 4 N.T.   You don't often try for a Grand Slam after a mere one-
          level opening, but partner has the two missing aces and
          good trump support. If he also has the two missing kings
          you must be able to make at least 6♠.

5. 3♣   After the positive response just rebid your own good
          suit. The inherent danger of partner being the first to
          bid in no-trumps is now nothing to worry about.

6. 7◊   Your hearts are not as self-supporting as in **6A**, No. 6,
          though responder's 4◊, of course, still shows long, solid
          and self-supporting diamonds missing the ace. Let him
          play in diamonds, as he will surely be able to ruff out
          your hearts if the suit doesn't fall.

Section 5

RESPONDER'S REBIDS
The Basic Rules

♠♡♣♢♠♡♣♢♠♡♣♢♠♡♣♢♠♡♣♢♠♡♣♢♠♡♣♢

WHEN responder's rebid in an uncontested auction has been reached there have already been three bids, and responder should be well on the way to knowing whether to settle for a part-score, game, or even a slam. If opener's rebid has been a sign-off or a limit bid, then responder is under no obligation to rebid himself. If he does so, therefore, it must be at least to improve, if not to increase the existing contract, though it may also be up to him to make further investigations as to the best final resting place.

1. On a Minimum Hand:

1♣—1NT When opener has made a sign-off rebid, responder may
2♣—No —and almost always should—now pass. Alternatively
 if opener has shown two suits, responder must show
1♣—1NT his preference, either by passing the second bid suit or
2♡—No returning opener to his first suit at the lowest available
or 2♠ level.

1♡—1♠ A repeat of responder's own suit at the lowest available
2♢—2♠ level is also a sign-off bid, showing weakness except
 for that suit and no particular liking for either of
 opener's suits.

1♣—2♣ If opener makes a trial bid in spite of responder's weak
3♢—3♣ limit bid, a minimum responding hand is shown by a
 simple rebid of opener's suit.

2. On a Better-than-Minimum Hand:

1♡—1♠ Responder may make another forward move as, for
2♢—2NT example, rebidding in no-trumps to show a count of
 10-12 pts. and a stop in the unbid suit.

1♡—1♠ A jump in responder's suit is encouraging, showing a
2♢—3♠ good suit and no particular interest in either of partner's
 suits.

1♡—1♠   A raise of partner's second suit or a jump bid in
2◇—3◇   partner's first suit constitutes a raise rather than mere
or 3♡   preference and also shows a better-than-minimum
hand.

1♠—2♠   Responder must also give a 'positive' response to
3◇—4♣   opener's trial bid if his original raise were made on
better than a minimum.

3. *Responding Hands with Game Hopes:*

1◇—1♡   On hands worth an attempt to reach a game contract
2◇—2♠   responder may 'reverse', a one-round force which
should be understood by opener as an invitation to
bid no-trumps if he holds the fourth (unbid) suit
stopped.

1♡—2◇   A new suit rebid at the three-level is also a one-round
2♡—3♣   force which may conveniently be used for exploration
with a no-trump contract in view.

1◇—1♡   A bid in the fourth suit is 'fourth suit forcing' con-
2♣—2♠   vention, used for exploration towards no-trumps or to
get opener to clarify his hand. Made at the two-level,
it does not guarantee a further bid if responder judges
that the best contract has now been reached. Opener,
in replying, should give priority to a rebid in no-trumps
at the appropriate level if holding a partial stop in the
fourth suit. The fourth-suit bid is a one-round force.

1♡—1♠   This again is fourth-suit-forcing, except that at the
2◇—3♣   three-level it guarantees a further bid if a game has not
been reached by opener's rebid.

1♡—2◇   If opener 'reverses', showing strength, responder should
2♠—?   aim at clarifying his hand, giving priority to a rebid in
no-trumps if holding the unbid suit covered.

1♡—3♡   Following the highly invitational limit bid of 3♡, a new
4♣—?   suit rebid by opener is a cue bid. Responder should,
unless minimum for his original three-level raise, show
his lowest-ranking first-round control in reply.

1♡—1♠   A return to opener's original suit after his 2 N.T. rebid
2NT—3♡   is forcing, requiring opener to bid 3 N.T. or the suit
game contract. As responder did not bid 3♡ in the
first place or 4♡ on this second round, opener can
expect no more than three-card trump support.

4. *On Strong Hands:*

1♡—1♠ 2♡—4♡	A delayed game raise sequence may be used when a hand is too strong for an initial limit bid at the three-level, as this might be passed out and a game missed,
1♡—1♠ 2NT—4♡	and not strong enough for an immediate forcing take-out. Compare the last example in No. 3 on p.135, where responder would rebid 4♡. In the third example
1♠—2♡ 2♠—4♠	sequence, responder will have a strong hand, but may have only three card trump support which can be deemed sufficient once opener's suit has been *re*bid.
1♠—2♢ 2♠—4♣	Even if responder has been unable to force initially, a subsequent jump bid in a new suit is still unconditionally forcing to game.
1♡—1♠ 2♡—2NT or 3 NT	Count-showing no-trump limit bids may also be made on suitable hands though a possibly more constructive initial response was made on the first round.
1♠—4♣ 4♢—?	When a responding hand has the requirements for a 'Swiss' response of 4♣ (four-card trump support, two aces, and 13-15 points), opener's rebid of 4♢ is a cue-bid
1♡—4♢ 4NT—?	Following either the 4♣ or 4♢ 'Swiss' response, any subsequent rebid of 4 N.T. by opener asks for kings, not aces which are already known, on the "Blackwood" scale.
1♠—3♢ 3♡—4♢	When responder is strong enough to make a game force on the first round, he should aim at clarifying his hand at his rebid. He knows that the auction will be kept
1♠—3♢ 3♣—4♠	open to game anyway. He may repeat his own suit, show support for opener's suit or perhaps rebid in no-trumps. Unless holding better than a minimum for his
1♢—3♣ 3♢—3NT	initial force, once having announced the strength to force, he should leave slam investigations to opener.

5. *Rebids Following a Strong Two Opening Bid:*

2♡—2NT 3♡—4♡ or No	After a negative response, opener's simple rebid in his original or in a second suit is not forcing. Responder may judge whether to pass or, even on a weak hand, make another move, knowing the strength held by his

2♠—2NT 3♡—No or 3♠ or 4♡ or 4♠	partner. If partner shows a two-suiter, responder must show preference, either by passing, correcting to the first-bid suit, or even possibly raising one or the other. These bids are a matter of common sense and judgement.
2♡—2NT 4◇—4♡ or 5◇	Opener's jump rebid in a new suit is forcing to game, and responder must either correct to the first suit or raise the second.
2♡—2NT 3♣—?	A 'reverse' rebid by opener is also forcing, and requires the same treatment.
2♡—3♣ 3♡—?	Any positive response makes the sequence forcing to game, and responder simply makes the most sensible rebid available.

6. Rebids Following a 2♣ Opening:

2♣—2◇ 2NT—?	2 N.T. is not forcing and responder may pass on a completely worthless hand. Similarly he is under no obligation to take action if opener rebids 3 N.T.
2♣—2◇ 2♡—?	A suit rebid by opener is unconditionally forcing to game. Responder's second negative is 2 N.T. which he must bid if common sense tells him he has no more constructive bid available.
2♣—2◇ 3♡—?	A jump rebid by opener asks responder to cue-bid any one ace he may possibly hold, in spite of his 2◇ negative.
2♣—2♡ 2♠—?	After any positive response to 2♣ the bidding proceeds naturally.

Section 5

RESPONDER'S REBIDS

Exercises

♠♡♣◇♠♡♣◇♠♡♣◇♠♡♣◇♠♡♣◇♠♡♣◇♠♡♣◇♠♡♣◇

THROUGHOUT this section you have already responded to your partner's opening bid, and in some cases to his subsequent bid. Now you have to decide on your rebid in each of the sequences shown.

No. 1　♠ 9　　　　　a) 1♡—2♡　　　b) 1♠—1 NT
　　　　♡ K 10 8 4　　　3◇—?　　　　2♣—?
　　　　◇ Q J 10 6
　　　　♣ 9 6 5 3

Answers : (a) Partner's 3◇ is a Trial Bid. It asks whether you are maximum or minimum for your 2♡ raise or, if you are doubtful, whether you can give any help in diamonds, a spot where he has some weakness. You are nearly maximum for your original bid and, in addition, you have 'help' in diamonds, so bid 4♡ direct.

(b) Opener's spades must be longer than his clubs, so he is almost certainly 5-4 in the two suits. You have, therefore, reached a sure 4-4 trump fit and, with no higher ambitions, you should pass this non-forcing rebid.

(Bids : 4♡ and No Bid.)

No. 2　♠ K J 7 4　　　a) 1♡—1♠　　　b) 1♡—1♠
　　　　♡ Q 9 3　　　　2♣—?　　　　2 NT—?
　　　　◇ K Q J 8
　　　　♣ 8 3

Answers : (a) With an honour to help in the suit opened by your partner and an excellent stop in the unbid suit, diamonds, rebid 2 N.T. This shows 10-12 pts. just as it would have done as an initial response except that, at that stage, clubs appeared to be wide open.

(b) Clearly you have the values to bid a game, but are not sure whether 3 N.T. or 4♡ will be best, the latter probably being the safer if partner has a five-card heart suit. Bid 3♡, a *forcing* bid (a return to opener's suit after his 2 N.T. rebid), requiring him to choose. He will know that you have neither the four-card trump support required for an immediate raise to 3♡, nor the values for a delayed game raise, with which you would now bid 4♡ yourself.

(Bids : 2 N.T. and 3♡.)

No. 3   ♠ 9 7 4   a) 1♠—1 NT   b) 1◇—2◇   c) 1♠—1 NT
       ♡ A Q 7   3◇—?   3♣—?   3◇—4◇
       ◇ J 9 6 3   4♠—?
       ♣ 7 4 3

Answers: (a) Opener's jump rebid is forcing which, in view of the fact that you could do no more than bid 1 N.T., must mean that he has a strong two-suiter. Do the obvious, which is to give him a raise to 4◇.

(b) 3♣ is a Trial Bid in the minors, and at least a one-round force. Rather than showing a weakness (as in No. 1 (a)), it shows a guard and asks whether partner can show another guard with the idea of getting into a final no-trump game contract. So bid 3♡, showing your strength in this department, which may be just what partner wants to hear.

(c) A game contract has now been reached so you are under no obligation to bid again and, indeed, should not do so. Three-card support for partner's bid and rebid suit is adequate and you have no slam ambitions.   (Bids : 4◇, 3♡, and No Bid.)

No. 4   ♠ K 10 9   a) 1♡—3♡   b) 1♠—2♣   c) 1♠—2♣
       ♡ 10 9 8 3   3♣—?   2♡—?   4♣—?
       ◇ 8
       ♣ A Q J 9 4

Answers: (a) 3♠ is a cue bid which means that your partner, in the light of your strong 3♡ limit bid, is now thinking in terms of a possible slam. Make a return cue bid of 4♣, not showing a club suit but showing first-round control of clubs, after which leave any further pressing to him.

(b) Never leave partner to do what you can do yourself—everything about your hand now looks good, so raise to 4♡.

(c) Doutbless you've found partner with a four-card club fit, but as he bid spades first that must be his longer suit, that is, at least a five-card suit. Put him to 4♠ and then, of course, follow up any further action he may possibly take.

                              (Bids : 4♣, 4♡, and 4♠.)

No. 5   ♠ Q 9 6 4   a) 1♡—2♡   b) 1♠—2♠   c) 1♢—1♡
        ♡ Q 10 8 3   3♢—?   3♡—?   2 NT—?
        ♢ 7 5 3
        ♣ K 5

Answers: (a) 3♢ is a Trial Bid again. However, if partner is looking for either a maximum for your original raise or help in diamonds, you have neither. Sign off in 3♡.

(b) 3♡ is also a Trial Bid, but there is a dfference when this is made in a *second major.* Partner may have a four-card heart suit, that is, he may be 5-4 in spades and hearts. As long as the rest of the hand justifies giving encouragement rather than a sign-off, you should raise the second major with a four-card fit for it, so here you should bid 4♡. With 'help' in the second major in the form of a shortage you would, of course, make the appropriate rebid in the original suit—for example, exchange your hearts and clubs, and you should bid 4♠ in response to the 3♡ Trial Bid.

(c) Notice how the same hand can demand positive or negative action according to partner's obvious requirements. Here, even if he has his 18 pt. maximum making a combined total of 25 pts., you have little with which to help him to go to town. Unless you are badly in need of points in a match, you would do best to pass.

(Bids : 3♡, 4♡, and No Bid.)

No. 6   ♠ K 9 6 4   a) 1♡—1♠   b) 1♡—1♠   c) 1♡—1♠
        ♡ A 8   2♣—?   2♢—?   2 NT—?
        ♢ Q 3 2
        ♣ K J 10 7

Answers: (a) If partner can help with even a partial stop in diamonds, 3 N.T. will surely be the best contract. *Ask* him with a fourth-suit forcing 2♢ which, as you will see, does *not* show a diamond suit.

(b) Unless so two-suited that you can't even think in terms of a no-trump contract, never go bidding away against your partner in your two suits whilst he bids the other two. Compare with (a) above where you asked about his diamond holding. Here show your excellent clubs and full values by bidding 3 N.T.

(c) Just raise to 3 N.T., for which clearly there must be ample points between the combined hands.

(Bids : 2♢, 3 N.T., and 3 N.T.)

No. 7   ♠ Q 5 4   a) 1♡—2♣   b) 1♠—3♣   c) 1♠—3♣
       ♡ 8   2♡—?   3♠—?   3◇—?
       ◇ A Q J 8
       ♣ A Q J 7 5

Answers : Note that because of the complete lack of heart fit, you content yourself with a simple 2♣ on the first round. When partner can only rebid 2♡ you bid 3◇, a responder's reverse as well as a new suit at the three-level and, therefore, forcing. With anything at all in spades your partner, who *must* bid again, will go into no-trumps.

(b) As ♠Q-x-x is by no means a lack of fit for partner's suit you force with 3♣ on the first round. When partner only rebids a neutral 3♠ raise to 4♠. Don't yourself go pressing on as he should be capable of taking the hint if he has anything like a decent hand.

(c) This time, with the almost incredible diamond rebid, you can afford to be the one to press on. Go straight into a 'Blackwood' 4 N.T., as you are perfectly prepared to play in a diamond slam if partner has the necessary controls.

(Bids : 3◇, 4♠, and 4 N.T.)

No. 8   ♠ A Q 10 9 7   a) 1◇—1♠   b) 1◇—1♠   c) 1◇—1♠
       ♡ A Q 9 7 4   2◇—?   1 NT—?   2♣—2♡
       ◇ 8   2 NT—?
       ♣ Q 3

Answers : (a) You can't afford not to try to reach the best game contract, so in spite of partner's apparent diamond sign-off, force with 3♡.

(b) If you are using a weak no-trump, partner is showing 15-16 pts. and again you want to find the best game contract. Bid 3♡.

(c) When partner's rebid was 2♣ you took your opportunity to bid a fourth-suit-forcing 2♡ which partner would take as a request to go into no-trumps if holding a partial guard in hearts. His confirmation that he has something in hearts can only mean that you have a reasonable heart fit, so bid 4♡—no one could expect you to want to play this hand in no-trumps.

(Bids : 3♡, 3♡, and 4♡.)

No. 9   ♠ A J 7 2   a) 1♡—2♣   b) 1♠—4♣   c) 1♠—4♣
        ♡ 8 5 3   2♠—?   4◇—?   4 NT—?
        ◇ 6
        ♣ A K 8 5 4

Answers : (a) Note that partner has made a forcing 'reverse' into 2♠, showing a strong hand with longer hearts than spades. The least you can do is bid 4♠, not as a shut-out, but to confirm the fit and your own excellent hand.

(b) Your 4♣ was 'Swiss', showing a four card trump fit, two aces, and 13-15 points. Partner's 4◇ is a cue bid to which you reply by showing your own *cheapest* control.

(c) Again, of course, your 4♣ was 'Swiss', and partner, therefore, already knows the number of aces you hold—two. He is now asking immediately if you have any kings in addition, and you respond 5◇ on the 'Blackwood' scale to show one.

(Bids : 4♠, 4♠, and 5◇.)

No. 10   ♠ A K 7 4   a) 1♡—4♣   b) 1♣—1♡   c) 1♣—1♡
        ♡ J 10 9 6   4 NT—?   2♣—?   2◇—?
        ◇ A 9 3
        ♣ Q 8

Answers: (a) Your 4♣ was 'Swiss', showing a four-card trump fit, two aces, and 13-15 points. Just as in No. 9 (c) above, partner is not asking something he already knows, so again he is asking for kings, if any, and you respond 5◇ to show one, on the 'Blackwood' scale.

(b) Go straight into 3 N.T. without further ado. Notice, by the way, that you bid the lower-ranking of your two four-card majors first.

(c) Whether or not an opener's 'reverse' in the second minor is unconditionally forcing or not is a controversial point. However, only on the weakest of weak responding hands would you think of passing. Bid your full values with 3 N.T. and leave it to opener to decide whether or not to go 'slamming'.

(Bids : 5◇, 3 N.T., and 3 N.T.)

No. 11 ♠ A Q 9 6 3   a) 1♠—3◇   b) 1♡—1♠   c) 1♡—1♠
     ♡ 10 7   3♡—?   2♡—?   3♡—?
     ◇ A K 9 6 2
     ♣ 6

Answers : (a) Having rightly forced on the first round don't bid your hand twice at this stage. Just rebid 3♠, knowing that partner is capable of understanding that you have the values for a force. You may well end up in a Grand Slam contract here.

(b) Not suitable for a first-round force when partner opened 1♡, you must still make an effort to reach the best game contract. Bid 3◇, a new suit at the three-level and, therefore, a one-round force. If partner can only rebid 3♡ raise him to 4♡, but if he rebids 3 N.T., stand it.

(c) Partner has shown a hand worth seven playing tricks at hearts, but note that he did not show eight playing tricks by opening 2♡. Don't be selfish—just raise to 4♡.

(Bids : 3♠, 3◇, and 4♡.)

No. 12 ♠ J 9 8 6   a) 1♡—1♠   b)   No   c)   No
     ♡ Q 7 3   2♣—?   1♣—?   1♣—1 NT
     ◇ A 9 4   2♠—?
     ♣ J 10 7

Answers : (a) Just give a simple preference bid of 2♡, not raising but, with even better heart than club support, putting him back to his first suit. His 2♣, of course, is not forcing, but it is still up to you to take action if appropriate.

(b) Having already passed—note this important fact—it is better to show a count of 8-10 pts. than to show this poor spade suit and risk a pass from partner.

(c) Opener is *not* making a forcing 'reverse', as your 1 N.T. is a strictly limited bid. He is, in fact, showing a black two-suiter, almost certainly five-five, which he doesn't fancy for a no-trump contract. Your hand is minimum for your first response and a good fit has been discovered, so pass.

(Bids : 2♡, 1 N.T., and No Bid.)

No. 13 ♠ K Q 10 7 4   a) 1♡—1♠   b) 1♡—1♠   c)   No
      ♡ K Q 8   2♡—?   2 NT—?   1♡—?
      ◇ J 9
      ♣ 9 7 4

Answers: (a) Give partner a chance by raising to 3♡. If his opening is absolutely minimum this might be unfortunate, but there has been no interference bidding so there is a good chance that he will be able to go on to 4♡ and make it.

(b) Your's not to guess whether 3 N.T. or 4♡ will be the better contract. Bid 3♡ (forcing, as it returns partner to his original suit after his 2 N.T. rebid). He will know you have good, though not four-card heart support and will bid either 3 N.T. or 4♡.

(c) Remember that a simple change-of-suit response after a previous pass is no longer forcing. With a near opener and a trump fit you can bid 2♠, not 1♠. 2♠ is a one-round force agreeing hearts as trumps, and opener must sign off in 3♡ or, if strong enough, bid 4♡.

(Bids : 3♡, 3♡, and 2♠.)

No. 14 ♠ Q J 8 7 5 4   a) 1♡—1♠   b) 1♣—1♠   c) 1♡—1♠
      ♡ 9 6 3   2♡—?   2♣—?   2◇—?
      ◇ K 8 4
      ♣ 6

Answers: (a) The sooner you pass, the better. Opener has not bid strongly and you have no hopes of a game. He might make 2♡, though, if your singleton club and ◇K fit in with his holdings.

(b) This time you have a singleton in partner's suit, not the useful three-card support you had in (a). Moreover your suit is a six-card major. Rebid 2♠, in itself a sign-off, which will yield a better score if you make it than 2♣ would do. If partner insists on playing in clubs now, he will know that he does so at his own peril !

(c) Though your diamond support is better in quality than your heart support, remember that partner may well be 5-4 in hearts and diamonds. Put him back to hearts as cheaply as possible.

(Bids : No Bid, 2♠, and 2♡.)

No. 15   ♠ K Q 10   a) 1♠—2♡   b) 1◇—1♡   c)   No
        ♡ K Q 8 6 5   3♡—?   2NT—?   1♠—?
        ◇ 10 7 3
        ♣ J 9

Answers: (a) Show delayed support for spades with a rebid of
3♠. Partner will know that you lack the four-card support necessary
for an immediate raise to 3♠, and also that you have not got
delayed game raise values. Leave the choice of final contract to
him.

(b) Raise to 3 N.T. Partner has shown 17-18 pts., and though you
have little in the minors, partner has bid diamonds and will surely
have something in clubs which your ♣J will help to 'boost'.

(c) This is virtually identical with the situation in No. 13 (c) the
point of which was that, once having passed, a simple change-of-
suit response is no longer forcing. So bid 3♡, showing a near
opener and agreeing spades as trumps. Partner will know you lack
four-card spade support, with which you would have bid 3♠, and
he will either convert 3♡ to 3♠, which you would pass, or he will
bid 4♠ direct.

(Bids : 3♠, 3 N.T., and 3♡.)

No. 16   ♠ K Q J   a) 1♠—2◇   b) 1♡—2◇   c) 1♣—1◇
        ♡ J 8 7 2   2 NT—?   2 NT—?   2 NT—?
        ◇ A Q 9 8 3
        ♣ 5

Answers :   (a) Here again you meet the situation where, lacking
four-card trump support, you wish to put the onus of deciding
between 3 N.T. and 4♠ onto your partner. This you do by making
a forcing rebid of 3♠. He will know that you have adequate, though
not four-card spade support, and the values for game somewhere.

(b) Being too strong for a first-round limit bid of 3♡, your 2◇
was intended as the preliminary to a delayed game raise. No onus
of any sort should be put on partner here—simply bid 4♡.

(c) As partner has now shown 17-18 pts., you can rest assured that
he has better than a three-card club suit (if you can't remember
why, refer back to Section 1, No. 15). So in spite of your club
singleton, raise to 3 N.T.

(Bids : 3♠, 4♡, and 3 N.T.)

No. 17 ♠ J 7 4   a) 1♣—2♣   b) 1◊—2♣   c) 1♡—2♣
       ♡ Q 9 3   2◊—?   2 NT—?   2♠—?
       ◊ 10 8
       ♣ A Q 7 6 3

Answers: (a) Neither your count nor your stop in hearts is good enough for a rebid in no-trumps at this stage, and nor are you strong enough to suggest a game contract by the use of a fourth-suit-forcing bid as you did in No. 6 (c). Just give quiet preference to 2♠ and leave it to partner who, after all, already knows you have eight points.

(b) Partner has shown a count of 15-16 pts., so between you you must have a minimum of 24, probably aided by your five-card suit. Raise to 3 N.T.

(c) Partner has made a forcing reverse, showing a strong hand with longer hearts than spades. As you *must* respond to this, you should give priority to showing a stop in the unbid suit if you can. With nothing in diamonds the sensible thing to do it to return partner to his first-bid suit by rebidding 3♡.

(Bids: 2♠, 3 N.T., and 3♡.)

No. 18 ♠ K Q 10 6   a) 1♡—1♠   b) 1◊—1♠   c) 1♠—2♣
       ♡ K J 9   2♡—?   2◊— 3 NT   2♠—?
       ◊ 7 6   4◊—?
       ♣ A J 7 3

Answers: (a) Your first response was automatic, but when partner rebids 2♡ you know that he has at least a five-card suit. Raise to 4♡ which must be an odds-on bet facing your own 14 pts.

(b) Any bid which removes an existing game contract to one below game, as 4◊ does, is *forcing*. Clearly partner has long diamonds but 5◊ is a long way to go and you have the other three suits well held. Bid 4 N.T. which, in view of your previous 3 N.T., followed by his take-out into 4◊, is not to be understood as 'Blackwood'. Partner can pass or rescue himself into 5◊.

(c) 2♣ was a waiting bid on a hand too good for 3♠ which might be passed or for a direct 4♠ which might cost a good slam. Make the delayed game raise to 4♠.

(Bids: 4♡, 4 N.T., and 4♠.)

No. 19 ♠ K J 10 9   a) 1♡—1♠   b) 1◇—1♠   c)   No
     ♡ Q 10 8   2♣—?   2 NT—?   1◇—?
     ◇ Q J 10 6
     ♣ 9 3

Answers :   (a) The quality of your hand is rather good for a sign-off into 2♡, and nor do you want to give jump preference to 3♡ until you are sure opener's heart suit is rebiddable. Temporise with 2 N.T. for which you are up to strength anyway.

(b) Even though partner has opened in a minor, a return to his original suit after his 2 N.T. rebid is forcing. Bid 3◇ from which he will understand that you have good diamond support though you made the possibly more constructive bid of 1♠ first. He will also realise that you have a weak spot somewhere (clubs), and he must now decide between bidding 3 N.T. or going on in diamonds.

(c) Once having passed originally, a 1♠ response would no longer be forcing though clearly this hand 'belongs' in diamonds. Bid an invitational 3◇, a limit bid, but partner will convert to 3 N.T. if he can.

                         (Bids : 2 N.T., 3◇, and 3◇.)

No. 20 ♠ Q 9 3 2   a) 1♡—3♡   b) 2♡—4♡   c) 2♣—2 NT
     ♡ K 7 4 3   4◇—?   4 NT—?   3◇—?
     ◇ K Q 6
     ♣ 8 4

Answers :   (a) 4◇ is a cue bid made in the light of your strong limit bid of 3♡. You have no additional values and no first-round controls, so sign off in 4♡.

(b) Your direct raise to 4♡ promised in the region of 9-10 pts. with no first-round controls, i.e. *no* ace or void. In spite of this partner is interested in a possible slam and he is now asking about kings on the 'Blackwood' scale. Bid 5♡ to show two.

(c) Your 2 N.T. was 'positive' denying nothing but a reasonably biddable suit. Simply agree trumps by raising to 4◇. Had the rebid been 3♣ you would have rebid 3 N.T.

                         (Bids : 4♡, 5♡, and 4◇.)

No. 21   ♠ 8 3   a) 1♣—1◇   b) 1♡—3♡   c) 1♠—2◇
       ♡ A J 8 7   1♡—?   3 NT—?   3♣—?
       ◇ K 10 7 5 4
       ♣ Q 6

Answers :   (a) Partner may have only a four-card heart suit and be taking his opportunity to show this at the one-level. However, had he opened 1♡ you would have raised to 3♡, so do this now.

(b) It is virtually certain that partner has only a four-card suit, but with your two doubletons the idea of playing in no-trumps is not attractive to you. You will never know before the hand is played whether 3 N.T. or 4♡ is better, but from your angle 4♡ looks the more promising, so bid it.

(c) 3♣, a new suit at the three-level is forcing, but don't make the mistake of bidding 3♡, busily showing both red suits when partner has the black ones. Bid 3 N.T. to show your heart stop.

(Bids : 3♡, 4♡, and 3 N.T.)

No. 22   ♠ A Q J 9 6   a) 1♡—1♠   b) 1◇—1♠   c) 2♡—3♡
       ♡ K J 8   2♣—?   2♣—?   4 NT—?
       ◇ Q 7
       ♣ 9 8 6

Answers :   (a) Bid a fourth-suit-forcing 2◇, asking for help in this department for a no-trump contract. Partner will give priority to a no-trump rebid, failing which he will choose the most expressive suit rebid, leaving you to decide the best final contract.

(b) Note the difference from (a) above, as this time you have an excellent guard in the fourth suit yourself. Bid 3 N.T., what your hand is worth.

(c) Note that trump agreement is more likely to help a partner who has opened with a Strong Two than a change-of-suit response. The single raise, unlike the direct raise to the four-level, promises *at least one* ace or void. 4 N.T. is, therefore, the 'Blackwood' request to show aces and you respond 5◇ to show one.

(Bids : 2◇, 3 N.T., and 5◇.)

No. 23   ♠ J 7   a) 1♠—2♣   b) 1◇—2♣   c) 2♠—3♣
       ♡ Q 8 2   2♡—?   4♣—?   3♡—?
       ◇ K J 5
       ♣ A Q 9 8 5

Answers : (a) Show your values and good diamond stop by a rebid of 3 N.T. A raise to 3♡ might be passed and a direct raise to 4♡ might land you in a 4-3 fit.

(b) Partner has deliberately by-passed the 3 N.T. level which means you are headed for a minor suit game or slam contract. Be as helpful as you can by bidding 4◇ to show diamond support.

(c) In a simple sequence such as (a) you rebid in no-trumps, but a partner with a two-suiter worth a Strong Two opening is not likely to be interested in a no-trump contract. Raise to 4♡ which is more likely to be helpful than a rebid of 3 N.T.

(Bids : 3 N.T., 4◇, and 4♡.)

No. 24   ♠ A Q J 9   a) 1♠—4♣   b) 1◇—1♡   c) 1♣—1♡
       ♡ K 10 9 4   4 NT—?   2◇—?   3◇—?
       ◇ 7 2
       ♣ A 8 5

Answers: (a) Your 'Swiss' 4♣ has already shown two aces, four-card trump support, and 13-15 points. Not asking a question to which he already knows the answer, therefore, partner is now enquiring about kings. Respond 5◇ on the 'Blackwood' scale to show one.

(b) You had the values for a first-round response of 3 N.T., but rightly chose the possibly more constructive and less cramping bid of 1♠. Bid 3 N.T. now, as you can't afford to be out of a game contract with 14 pts. facing an opening bid.

(c) In the light of partner's forcing rebid you are far too strong to rebid 3 N.T. Bid 4♣, by-passing the 3 N.T. level. Compare this hand with No. 21 (c) where your initial response had already shown a minimum of 8 pts.

No. 25 ♠ A K 6   a) 1♣—1♡   b) 1♢—1♡   c) 1♣—1♡
      ♡ K Q 10 7 6   2♣—?   2♣—?   1♠—2♢
      ♢ 8 3   2 NT—?
      ♣ J 9 3

Answers: (a) The best rebid here is 2♠, a 'responder's reverse' and a one-round force. It shows a good stop in the reverse-bid suit and though it might even show a second suit, it guarantees a good hand able to stand preference to the original suit at the three-level. Opener should give priority to a rebid in no-trumps if he can stop the fourth suit. Obviously opener must not give enthusiastic raises to the reverse-bid suit, but should treat it as exploration towards a no-trump contract.

(b) Bid a fourth-suit-forcing 2♠ to get opener to clarify his hand, after which you will be in a good position to judge the best final contract.

(c) Your fourth-suit-forcing 2♢ has been given confirmation that partner holds something in diamonds. Raise now to 3♠, telling him that 3 N.T. was not necessarily your final goal, leaving him to choose between spades and no-trumps.

(Bids: 2♠, 2♠, and 3♠.)

No. 26 ♠ K J 7 2   a) 1♡—1♠   b) 2♣—4♠   c) 2♣—2♠
      ♡ K J 6   2♢—?   5♢—?   2 NT—?
      ♢ 8 4
      ♣ K 6 5 3

Answers: (a) Your choice lies between a raise to 3♡ (not mere preference to 2♡) or a rebid of 2 N.T. to show your count and club stop. The latter is the better choice.

(b) Partner is making a slam try which, as he knows you have no ace or void, must mean that he has at least three first-round controls himself. Respond by showing the cheapest second-round control you have, 5♡, which he will know is either the king or a singleton.

(c) You would—and did—bid 1♠ over 1♡, as in (a) and equally, with a hand worth a positive response to 2♣, you can show even a modest suit at the two-level. Now opener rebids 2 N.T. showing 23-24 pts. Raise direct to 6 N.T. knowing you have a combined minimum count of 34 pts.

(Bids: 2 N.T., 5♡, and 6 N.T.)

No. 27 ♠ A K J 9 8   a) 1♡—2♣   b) 3♣—3♠   c) 3♡—4◇
       ♡ K J 9   2♡—3◇   4♣—?   4♡—?
       ◇ A K J 10   3♡—?
       ♣ 4

Answers: (a) Partner has signed off as clearly as he can. Never-
theless you know about your heart fit, singleton club, and outside
strength. You won't be bidding your hand twice if you now press
on to 4 N.T., as with even one ace in his hand, 6♡ becomes a good
proposition.

(b) Your change-of-suit response, even to a pre-emptive three-
bid, is a one-round force. Made in a major suit, it shows a good suit
which partner may raise on a doubleton-queen or three small. In
view of his original 3♣ opening, settle for the game contract by
passing.

(c) A change-of-suit response in a *minor* should be understood
as a slam try, probably in the suit opened. In view of your heart fit
you must now ask whether partner has even one ace, as you are
willing to play in 5♡ if he has none.

(Bids : 4 N.T., No Bid, and 4 N.T.)

No. 28 ♠ K J 7   a) 2◇—3 NT   b) 2♣—2 NT c) 2◇—3 NT
       ♡ K J 4   4 NT—?   3◇—?   4◇—?
       ◇ 9 8 3
       ♣ Q 10 8 6

Answers: (a) 3 N.T. shows 10-12 points, with no biddable suit. It
would be senseless to regard partner's 4 N.T. as quantative in this
situation, so it must be a request for you to show aces. With none,
of course, you respond 5♣ on the 'Blackwood' scale.

(b) With 10 pts. you are too good for an initial 2◇ response,
but partner's 3◇ rebid shows the one suit for which you have no
active support. Rebid 3 N.T.

(c) Partner's 4◇, which removes an existing game contract to one
below game level, is forcing. Just raise to 5◇ if that's the way he
wants it—he already knows the sort of hand you have.

(Bids : 5♡, 3 N.T., and 5◇.)

No. 29 ♠ Q 9 7 2 a) 1♠—2♠ b) 2♠—3♠ c) 4 NT—5♡
     ♡ A J 3   3♣—?   4♣—?   5♠—?
     ◇ 7 6
     ♣ 9 8 7 4

Answers : (a) You can't confirm 'help' in clubs or a maximum 2♠ raise in response to partner's 3♣ Trial Bid. Compromise by making a 'passing the buck' bid of 2♡ showing where you have some values.

(b) Having guaranteed at least one ace or void by your 3♠ bid, partner is now angling to discover just what you have got. Unlike the 3♣ bid in (a), 4♣ is a cue bid. Respond by a cue bid of your own ace, 4♡.

(c) Many people forget that a 4 N.T. opening does NOT call for 'Blackwood' responses. With no ace you bid 5♣, with one ace you cue-bid the suit (6♣ for the ♣A) and with two aces bid 5 N.T. Your's not to reason why he bid 4 N.T., but you have responded truthfully, after which you must pass any rebid he makes, as this will be his decision as to the final contract.

(Bids : 3♡, 4♡, and No Bid.)

No. 30 ♠ K J 6 a) 1♣—1 NT b) 1♡—2 NT c) 1♣—1 NT
     ♡ J 9 8   2 NT—?   3◇—?   2♠—?
     ◇ Q 9 8
     ♣ K 9 5 2

Answers : (a) Three easy ones to end with. First, having shown 8-10 pts. by bidding 1 N.T., your partner is now inviting 3 N.T. Having your full 10 pt. maximum, go to 3 N.T.

(b) A trifle under strength for your initial 2 N.T., which was the lesser evil than the possible alternatives, you are now faced with a forcing rebid. 5◇ seems a highly dangerous contract, so rebid 3 N.T.

(c) This is not a forcing 'reverse', as doubtless partner intended to rebid a simple 1♠ over a red suit response. He must, therefore, have a black two-suiter which he doesn't fancy for no-trumps and both must be at least five-card suits. Give him 3♠, confirming spade support and a maximum for your 1 N.T.

(Bids : 3 N.T., 3 N.T., and 3♠.)

Section 5

RESPONDER'S REBIDS
Competition Quiz

IN competition against another player, each in turn should answer a full page of six questions. As an added exercise you might like to decide on the correct first-round response before going on to the scoring questions on responder's rebids. You met all the original responses in Section 2 and now you are asked to name your next bid in each of the auctions shown.

1A.

1. ♠ K J 7 2
♡ 9 8 6 5
◇ 9 3
♣ Q J 10

  1◇—1♠
  2♣—?

2. ♠ K J 8 2
♡ Q 10 7
◇ 9 5
♣ K Q J 3

  1♡—1♠
  2◇—?

3. ♠ K J 7 2
♡ Q 10 8 3
◇ J 8 6
♣ 10 8

  1♣—1♡
  1♠—?

Answer:
Bid (2 pts.)   Reason (3 pts.)

1. **No Bid** Your hand is worth only one bid (unless you find yourself required to show 'preference' by a rebid). Here show your preference for clubs by passing.

2. **2 N.T.** Show your club stop and 10-12 pts. with this limit bid.

3. **No Bid** First check back to Section 2, No. 8, if you failed to get the correct first response here and on No. 1. In both these hands you had the values for only one forward-going bid and here, when partner's rebid comes in a suit for which you have an excellent fit, you pass.

What would you bid next on the same hands in these sequences?

4. 1♡—2♡
   3◇—?

5. 1♡—1♠
   2 NT—?

6. 1◇—1♡
   2♣—?

Answer:
Bid (2pts.)   Reason (3 pts.)

4. **3♡** 3◇ is a Trial Bid and, therefore, a one-round force. Even with diamond 'help' your hand is too poor to do more than sign off.

5. **3 N.T.** Opener has shown 17-18 pts. which your hand more than adequately makes up to game values.

6. **2◇** This is a simple preference bid and *not* a raise.

1B.

1. ♠ K J 7 2	2. ♠ K J 6	3. ♠ J 9 8 6
♡ K 10 8 4	♡ 9 6 5 3	♡ Q 10 8 4
◇ A 6 2	◇ A Q J 8 3	◇ K 8
♣ 10 6	♣ 7	♣ 7 6 2
1◇—1♡	1♠—2◇	1◇—1♡
2♣—?	2◇—?	2♣—?—

Answers:

Bid (2 pts.)   Reason (3 pts.)

1. 2 N.T. Note the initial 1♡ bid, on a hand good enough for
another bid if partner signs off in 2◇. Now, with a
good spade stop and 10-12 pts., show your count.

2. 4♡ Had partner opened 1♡ you would have used a delayed
game raise sequence via 2◇ to ensure a 4♡ contract.
Now, when he rebids in hearts, you must show your full
values and four-card fit by a jump to 4♡.

3. No Bid Note the original 1♡ response on this weak hand
with two four-card majors. Show your club preference
by passing.

What would you bid next on the same hands in these sequences?

4. 1♡—3♡	5. 1♡—2◇	6. 1♠—2♠
4♣—?	3♣—?	3◇—?

Answers:

Bid (2 pts.)   Reason (3 pts.)

4. 4◇ 4♣ is a cue bid showing first round control, which must
mean that opener is making a slam try. Make a cost-
nothing return cue bid showing, not a diamond suit, but
a control.

5. 4♡ 3♣, a new suit at the three-level, is forcing. Show your
heart fit and strength by a jump to 4♡, not a mere 3♡.

6. 3♠ Even though partner makes a hopeful trial bid and you
have 'help' for him in that department, your hand is
too weak to do more than sign off by returning him
to 3♠.

2A.

1. ♠ K Q 9 3
♡ 10 7 4
◇ A 6 4
♣ K J 10

1♡—1♠
2◇—?

2. ♠ K Q 10 9 7 3
♡ 8 4
◇ 7 5
♣ J 6 4

1♡—1♠
2◇—?

3. ♠ Q 10 7
♡ 5
◇ A Q J 8 4
♣ A Q J 6

1♡—2◇
2♡—?

Answers:
Bid (2 pts.)   Reason (3 pts.)

1. 3 N.T.   Bid your own cards and don't wait for partner to bid
them for you! With 14 pts. (two tens) and an excellent
club stop the least you can do is go straight to 3 N.T.

2. 2♠   Your own suit is good enough to rebid in preference to
passing 2◇ or putting partner back to 2♡.

3. 3♣   Your failure to force originally was due to lack of heart
fit, but even when partner signs off you must press on in
an attempt to find the best game contract. 3♣, a new
suit at the three-level, is a one-round force and if
partner can show some holding in spades with 3 N.T.,
you will be happy to pass.

What would you bid next on the same hands in these sequences?

4. 1♡—1♠
2♣—?

5. 1♡—1♠
3 NT—?

6. 1♡—2◇
2♡—3♣
4◇—?

Answers:
Bid (2 pts.)   Reason (3 pts.)

4. 2◇   You feel sure that between you, you have game values,
but are *not* sure as to the best final denomination. Get
partner to clarify his hand by bidding a 'fourth suit
forcing' 2◇. With as much as ◇Q-x he will rebid in
no-trumps. If he bids 2 N.T. you will raise to 3 N.T.
which, with the lead coming up to his hand, should be
the best bet.

5. 4♠   This is likely to be much safer than 3 N.T.

6. 5◇   Partner has denied even a partial spade guard so you
would bid no-trumps at your peril! However, he is
likely to have at least three-card diamond support, so
go for 5◇.

2B.

1. ♠ 7	2. ♠ J 9	3. ♠ 7 4
♡ Q 9 2	♡ J 7 4	♡ 9
◇ A Q J 8	◇ A Q 10 9 3	◇ A Q 10 9 7 6 4
♣ A J 10 9 3	♣ K J 6	♣ Q 6 2
1♡—2♣	1♠—2◇	1♣—1◇
2 NT—?	2♡—?	2NT—?

Answers:

Bid (2 pts.)   Reason (3 pts.)

1. 3♡   You are obviously nervous of a no-trump contract, but
if opener has only a four-card heart suit . . . ? Bid a
forcing 3♡, leaving the choice between 3 N.T. and 4♡
to partner. He will know that he is not getting four-card
heart support from you.

2. 2 N.T.   This, of course, promises a club guard—the unbid suit.

3. 3◇   Sign off in your own long suit, the only one that appeals
to you as trumps, at the same time showing no game
ambitions.

What would you bid next on the same hands in these sequences?

4. 1♠—2♣	5. 1♣—1◇	6. 1♡—2◇
2♡—?	1♠—?	3♣—?

Answers:

Bid (2 pts.)   Reason (3 pts.)

4. 3 N.T.   You have an extremely good holding in diamonds, the
unbid suit. Never mind your singleton—partner's bid
this suit. Bid your full values, 3 N.T., not a mere 2 N.T.

5. 2♡   A 'fourth-suit-forcing' bid, asking partner to clarify his
hand. With even a partial heart guard he will give
priority to a rebid in no-trumps. 2♡ is forcing for one
round, so if you don't like partner's answer the sequence
can stop below game level.

6. 3◇   3♣, a new suit at the three-level, is a one-round force
asking *you* to clarify your hand. You can do nothing
except repeat your diamonds.

3A.

1. ♠ J 10 7 4	2. ♠ A 8 6 3	3. ♠ J 9 2
♡ A 10	♡ A 7 5	♡ A Q 3
◇ A Q J 10 8 4	◇ 9 2	◇ A Q 10 7 4
♣ 8	♣ K Q J 7	♣ Q 9
1♣—1◇	1♣—1♠	1♠—2◇
1♠—?	2♡—?	2♠—?

Answers:

Bid (2 pts.)   Reason (3 pts.)

1. **4♠**   Had partner opened 1♠ you would have taken definite steps to make sure at least a game contract was reached. He will not take a jump to 4♠ as a sign-off but as strength-showing.

2. **3◇**   A fourth-suit-forcing bid as you are not yet sure of the best possible game contract. 3◇ also promises one further bid if this is necessary to reach game so opener need not jump to game at this stage.

3. **4♠**   Once partner has rebid his spades, this should be the best final contract, particularly as you now know that he is not strong enough to bid any more forcefully.

What would you bid next on the same hands in these sequences?

4. 1♠—4♣	5. 1♠—4♣	6. 1♠—2◇
4◇—?	4 NT—?	2♡—?

Answers:

Bid (2 pts.)   Reason (3 pts.)

4. **4♡**   Your 4♣ was 'Swiss' showing a trump fit, two aces, and 13-15 points, and the 4◇ rebid is a cue bid—it is *not* showing a diamond suit! Cue-bid your own cheapest control.

5. **5◇**   Your 4♣ was 'Swiss' showing a trump fit, two aces, and 13-15 points. As partner already knows you have two aces, he is asking for kings, and you show one on the 'Blackwood' scale.

6. **3♣**   Mark time with a fourth-suit forcing bid to see whether, in clarifying his hand, partner rebids one of his majors, after which you can put him to game in it. Remember you promise one further bid, so if he rebids 3♡ or 3♠ you will raise.

3B.

1. ♠ A 10 9 3	2. ♠ A J 10 7 4	3. ♠ K J 8
♡ Q 10 8	♡ J 10 7 3	♡ Q 10 8
◇ 7	◇ 6	◇ A J 9 7 6
♣ A K Q 6 3	♣ A K 6	♣ 7 6
1♠—3♣	1◇—1♠	1♡—2◇
3♠—?	2♣—?	2♠—?

Answers:

Bid (2 pts.)   Reason (3 pts.)

1. **4♠**   Don't fall into the temptation of bidding your hand twice by yourself pressing on for a slam. Opener knows you have the strength to force, and now he knows you can support spades, *he* may be able to go on.

2. **3 N.T.**   With any luck partner has five in either minor and your ♣A-K should make this good for five tricks (surely four). You must have a guard in hearts and he has diamonds while you have spades. Don't bid 2 N.T. on 13 pts., when this might be passed.

3. **4♡**   Partner has 'reversed' showing a strong hand with hearts longer than spades, which makes ♡Q-10-8 very adequate support. 3♡ would be a mere preference, when you have the values for game.

What would you bid next on the same hands in these sequences?

4. 1♡—3♣	5. 1♡—4♣	6. 1♠—2◇
3♡—?	4 NT—?	2♡—?

Answers:

Bid (2 pts.)   Reason (3 pts.)

4. **4♡**   As in No. 1 above, leave it to opener to decide whether to go on for a slam or not. He will have got the message that you have the strength to force, but you have not got much extra to this.

5. **5◇**   As in No. 4 on the previous page, your 4♣ was 'Swiss' showing a trump fit, two aces, and 13-15 points. Partner now asks how many kings you have—show one.

6. **3♠**   A raise, as distinct from a preference, to partner's first bid suit. Compare No. 3 on the previous page where you yourself had a partial club stop, so were interested in a possible no-trump game contract.

4A.

1.	2.	3.
♠ A 10 8 3	♠ A 10 9 7 5	♠ A J 10 6
♡ Q J 9 4	♡ Q 7 4	♡ K 10 9 4
◇ 7 6	◇ 6	◇ 7 2
♣ A 9 3	♣ A K 9 4	♣ K 6 3
1♡—4♣	1♡—1♠	1♣—1♡
4 NT—?	2♡—?	2◇—?

Answers:

Bid (2 pts.)   **Reason (3 pts.)**

1. **5♣**   Your 4♣ was 'Swiss' again, so as opener already knows you have two aces, he is asking if you have any kings. Respond 5♣ to show none—the 'Blackwood' scale.

2. **4♡**   Once partner rebids his hearts you can raise direct to game. There is no need to investigate further.

3. **3 N.T.**   Whether or not opener's minor suit reverse is forcing is one of those arguable points, though many expert players would take it as forcing. At least it must be very highly invitational. With the good spade holding, go to game in no-trumps. Note, by the way, the original heart response.

What would you bid next on the same hands in these sequences?

4. 1◇—1♡	5. 1♡—1♠	6. 1♡—3♡
2♣—?	4♠—?	4◇—?

Answers:

Bid (2 pts.)   Reason (3 pts.)

4. **2 N.T.**   Again note the original heart response. Show your 10-12 pts. and spade stop with the 2 N.T. limit bid.

5. **4 N.T.**   Partner sounds as though he has 'reversing' values in hearts and spades. An immediate slam try is the only possible response—remember that 4♠ is not a shut-out but intended to make sure that at least a game contract is reached.

6. **4♠**   Partner must be angling for a slam contract as he is now making a cue bid. You are maximum for your original 3♡ so make a return cue bid of 4♠, even though this must drive the contract to at least 5♡. But almost for certain the ♠A is what opener is hoping you will have.

4B.

1. ♠ K J 9 7 5	2. ♠ K Q 9 7 5	3. ♠ K Q 9 7 5
♡ K 9 8 4	♡ K J 10 9	♡ A 9
◇ J 6 3	◇ J 6 3	◇ J 6 3
♣ 8	♣ Q	♣ Q 7 2
1◇ —1♠	1◇—1♠	1◇—1♠
2♣—?	2♣—?	2♣—?

Answers:

Bid (2 pts.)   Reason (3 pts.)

1. 2◇   Compare these three hands carefully. In the first you are not strong enough to investigate a no-trump contract in spite of your heart stop, so just give preference to 2◇.

2. 2 N.T.   Here you *don't* go bidding against your partner in the majors while he bids the minors. Show your values and good—even biddable in different circumstances—heart suit with 2 N.T.

3. 2♡   This time a genuine fourth-suit forcing bid of 2♡ will show interest in the best game contract—no-trumps if partner can help with hearts. So make sure you understand that a bid in the fourth suit, until developments of the auction show otherwise, *asks* about that suit but doesn't *show* it.

What would you bid next on the same hands in these sequences?

4. 1♣—1♠	5. 1♡—1♠	6. 1♡—1♠
3 NT—?	2◇—?	2♣—?

Answers:

Bid (2 pts.)   Reason (3 pts.)

4. No Bid   Partner is showing 19 pts. and either your spade bid has done something to fill a gap or all he needed was to know you could respond, if only at the one-level. Pass and leave him to play.

5. 4♡   You had a first-round choice of 1♠ or an immediate 4♡ (being too good for 3♡). Now give a delayed game rise to 4♡.

6. 2◇   Once again fourth-suit-forcing comes to the rescue, not showing diamonds but asking about them, as if partner can help to 'boost' your ◇J into a stop, 3 N.T. is likely to be the best game contract. But a two-level fourth suit bid does not commit you to bid again if you don't like what you hear.

5A.
1. ♠ 6 3 2 2. ♠ A K 9 7 5 3. ♠ J 9 8 6
   ♡ A J 10 6   ♡ A Q 8 6 3   ♡ K 6 2
   ◇ 7   ◇ J 7   ◇ J 10 4
   ♣ A K 7 5 4   ♣ 6   ♣ A 7 5

   1♣—2♣   1◇—1♠   1♡—1♠
   2◇—?   2♣—?   2♣—?

Answers: Bid (2 pts.)   Reason (3 pts.)

1. 3 N.T. Don't bid against partner by showing clubs and hearts while he has spades and diamonds. 3 N.T. should be the best contract.

2. 2♡   You may think that, now you are familiar with fourth-suit-forcing, life is difficult for you here. Not a bit of it—remember the comment in **4B.**, No. 3. Bid 2♡ and await the coming developments.

3. 2♡   Simple preference to partner's first suit is all you can bid. If your four-card suit had been any other than one you could show at the one-level you would have bid 1 N.T. in the first place.

What would you bid on the same hands in these sequences?

    4. 1♡—4♣   5. 1◇—1♠   6.   No
      4 NT—?   2♣—2♡   1♣—?
                 2 NT—?

Answers: Bid (2 pts.)   Reason (3 pts.)

4. 5◇   What a difference the 1♡ opening makes to the bidding of this hand! Now you have a first-round 'Swiss' response. Show one king on the 'Blackwood' scale in response to his 4 N.T.

5. 4♡   Partner has, of course, taken your 2♡ as fourth-suit forcing and has replied showing at least a partial guard in the suit. This means a partial fit, perhaps ♡K-x or ♡J-x-x and as no one could expect you to want to play this two-suiter in no-trumps if a suit contract can be discovered, bid 4♡.

6. 1 N.T. Having already passed it is better to show your count of 8-10 points than to bid 1♠, a suit in which you are not extremely anxious to be left to play, even at the one-level.

5B.

1. ♠ K Q 9 8 6
♡ K J 9
◇ J 10 5
♣ 7 4

1♡—1♠
2 NT—?

2. ♠ Q 8
♡ 9 3
◇ 7 4
♣ A K Q J 10 8 5

1♡—2♣
2◇—?

3. ♠ K J 10 6 4
♡ A 10
◇ 6 2
♣ A J 8 5

1♡—1♠
2◇—?

Answers:

Bid (2 pts.)   Reason (3 pts.)

1. 3♡   In search of the best game contract, has partner got a four or five-card heart suit—will 4♡ be better than 3 N.T.? Ask with a forcing 3♡ (a return to opener's suit after his 2 N.T. rebid), which requires him to make the choice. He will not expect four-card heart support as you could not bid an immediate 3♡ in the first place.

2. 2♠   5♣ is a long way to go and 3 N.T. would be a pure 'shoot'. Ask partner if he can help with something in spades as well as his red suits, with a fourth-suit-forcing 2♠.

3. 3 N.T.   No need to ask about anything here—just settle for 3 N.T. which your hand is worth. You need no help to stop clubs.

What would you bid on the same hands in these sequences?

4. 1◇—1♠
   2♣—?

5. 2♡—4♣
   4♡—?

6. 1♣—1♠
   2♠—?

Answers:

Bid (2 pts.)   Reason (3 pts.)

4. 2 N.T.   Only 10½ pts., but you must show the heart stop in this hand, which is certainly worth another forward-going move.

5. No Bid   Your 4♣ was conventional, showing a solid and self-supporting club suit, but partner is still not interested. He must know that two aces are missing or that he has a likely heart loser as well as one missing ace. Trust his judgement.

6. 4♠   With a hand worth a 1♠ opening in the first place a spade game contract is the obvious one. As it doesn't look slam-worthy, just bid what you expect to make.

6A.

1. ♠ 9 4	2. ♠ K 9 8 4	3. ♠ K J 7
♡ K J 8	♡ Q 6 3	♡ K 9 3 2
◇ K J 7 2	◇ Q 10 9 2	◇ —
♣ K 6 3 2	♣ 6 5	♣ Q J 9 7 6 2
2♡—4♡	2♣—2◇	2♠—3♣
4 NT—?	2♠—?	4♣—?

Answers:

Bid (2 pts.)   Reason (3 pts.)

1. **5♣**   Don't forget that by your jump to 4♡ you denied any first-round conrol; so partner already knows you are aceless, and he is asking for your kings on the 'Blackwood' scale.

2. **4♠**   Partner already knows you could do no better than an initial 2◇ response. The jump to 4♠ now shows scattered strength below 'positive' requirements—which you have—no ace or void, and good trump support. This bid is, of course, a modified version of the direct raise to the four-level facing a Strong Two.

3. **4◇**   Note the single raise in a hand which contains good trump support and a first-round control—the diamond void. When partner cue-bids the clubs (very possibly a void of his own), cue bid your diamond void.

What would you bid on the same hands in these sequences?

4. 2♠—3 NT	5. 2♣—2◇	6. 2♠—3♠
4 NT—?	3♣—?	4◇—?

Answers:

Bid (2 pts.)   Reason (3 pts.)

4. **5♣**   The 3 N.T. response to 2♠ conventionally shows about 10-11 pts., and no biddable suit. 4 N.T. here should be taken as 'Blackwood', for what other means has opener by which to go slamming if he wants to find out more about your hand?

5. **3 N.T.**   The suit rebid, even though clubs, makes the sequence forcing to game. Neither of your four card suits is worth suggesting as trumps and you can't support clubs, so bid 3 N.T.

6. **4♠**   This is a pity, because you now know that your diamond void is duplication of values as partner must be showing the ace. You have no other control to show, so sign off in 4♠.

6B.

1. ♠ Q 9 7 6	2. ♠ K J 9 7 6	3. ♠ K 6 3
♡ A Q J	♡ 8 4	♡ 8 4
◇ J 10 9	◇ A J 2	◇ K J 9 7 6
♣ J 10 8	♣ J 10 8	♣ J 10 8
2♠—3♣	2♡—2♠	2♡—2 NT
4♣—4♡	3◇—?	3♣—?
4♠—?		

Answers:

Bid (2 pts.)   Reason (3 pts.)

1. No Bid Your 3♣ showed at least one ace or void, not one only, 4♣ was a cue bid to which you respond by showing your lowest-ranking control, so you have *denied* control of diamonds. Trust partner's judgement when he signs off.

2. 4◇ Your first response was 'positive', showing a suit and no reasonable heart support. Partner has now shown a second red suit and the least you can do is tell him that you like his second offer.

3. 3◇ With only a negative response on the first round, you are not particularly interested in either of partner's suits though you have too much not to try to help him into a game contract. Show your biddable suit.

What would you bid next on the same hands in these sequences?

4. 2♣—2 NT	5. 2♣—2♠	6. 2♠—2 NT
3♣—?	2 NT—?	3♣—?

Answers:

Bid (2 pts.)   Reason (3 pts.)

4. 4♠ Don't hurry it—you've already made a positive response. Now just show that you like his suit and leave it to him—he can't fail to go 'slamming'.

5. 6 N.T. Partner is showing 23-24 pts., as he would be doing by a 2 N.T. rebid after 2◇ from you. You have a five-card suit as well as the points to bring your combined hands into the Little Slam range, so bid it.

6. 4♠ Your hand was too modest to give an initial positive response, but you would be understating it badly if you gave a mere preference bid of 3♠ now. ♠K-x-x is adequate support, and partner already knows you haven't got much.

Section 6
CONTESTED AUCTIONS
The Basic Rules

♣♡♣♢♠♡♣♢♠♡♣♢♠♡♣♢♠♡♣♢♠♡♣♢♠♡♣♢

It is clearly beyond the scope of this book to attempt to cover all competitive situations, but the following details will give the student some guiding principles on which to base his bidding in many of the more usual situations. Emphasis is given to the possible difference an enemy opening or intervening bid can make.

1. *Immediate Overcalls:*

W.   N.   E.   S.

1♡—1♠   At the one-level, and particularly when not vulnerable, an overcall need not be very strong. Even if doubled and left to play, a one-level contract takes a lot of defeating to make it a worthwhile exchange for a declarer score. For a one-level intervention you should be able to estimate four playing tricks if not vulnerable, or five if vulnerable. A five-card suit.

1♡—2♢   At the two-level, playing strength is of great importance, and unless a six-card suit is held there should be adequate compensating honour strength. You should be able to estimate five playing tricks if not vulnerable and six if vulnerable.

1♡—1 N.T.   An intervening 1 N.T. is strong, the barest minimum being 15 pts. including a double stop in the enemy's suit.

1♡—Dbl   This is a request to partner to take out into his own best suit. Should be used on hands on which it seems wiser to discuss the final trump suit with partner rather than tell him your own good suit. Partner's responses are set out in No. 6 on p. 168.

1♡—2♠
or
1♠—3♣   Next in strength, on a 'shape' hand, comes a jump in a new suit. This shows a good playable suit of at least six-card length, in a hand too good for a simple overcall at the lowest available level. It is highly invitational but not forcing.

W.	N.	E.	S.	
		1♡	2♡	An immediate cue-bid of the suit opened shows a 'shape' hand even stronger than the jump overcall. It is a game force and may be used on a strong single or two-suited hand. Knowing the strength facing him, partner will keep open to game showing 4-card suits in ascending order.

2. Re-Opening in the 'Protective' Position:

W.	N.	E.	S.	
1♡	—	—	1♠	Fourth-in-hand after two passes, South should reopen the bidding competitively if possible, as once opener's partner has passed (and is, therefore, known to be extremely weak) there is a good chance that North has a share of the outstanding values even though he could not intervene immediately—possibly because of a good holding in the suit opened. The weakest protective bid, a change-of-suit at the one-level, can be made on as little as 8 or 9 pts. and a biddable suit.
1♡	—	—	2◇	A protective bid at the two-level shows at least a five-card suit and better than 8 or 9 pts.
1♡	—	—	2♣	A jump bid in a new suit shows a good hand with a good playable suit and a wish to contest for a part-score or even possibly a game.
1♠	—	—	1 NT	This shows 11-15 pts. and a stop in the suit opened. Note the difference from an immediate 1 N.T. overcall.
1◇	—	—	Dbl	Shows 9 or more with tolerance for any suit into which partner may take out or on which South would not be dismayed to defend if North converts to a business double by passing.
1♣	—	—	2♣	A cue bid of the suit opened is 'forcing to suit agreement' which means that it may be used on relatively weak hands of suitable shape (4-4-4-1 with a singleton in the

suit opened is ideal), as the bidding can be dropped below game once a suit fit has been discovered. If the cue-bidder's hand is strong, therefore, it is up to him to bid on.

A player responding to a 'protective' bid must remember the low values which may be held by partner and respond accordingly.

3. *Responding to a Suit Intervening Bid:*

W.	N.	E.	S.	
1♡	1♠	—	2♢	A simple change-of-suit response to partner's intervening bid is *not* forcing, for
1♡	2♢	—	3♢	which reason South should give priority to a raise of North's bid suit if this is possible, leaving a change-of-suit bid as a denial of support for North's suit. Other bids in South's position are largely a matter of common sense, but see No. 7 on p. 169., Directional Asking Bids.

4. *Responding After on Intervening Bid:*

W.	N.	E.	S.	
	1♠	2♢	2♠ or 3♠	Suit limit bids are unaffected by an intervening bid, and should be given to the full values held.
	1♠	2♢	2 NT or Dbl	In the case of no-trump limit bids in response, the same values as in an uninterrupted sequence are shown but a good stop in the suit intervened is also guaranteed. Probably better to make a business double.
	1♠	—	2♣ But	A suit intervention by East may obstruct South's change-of-suit response if he is good enough to bid at the two-level but not at the three-level. It may then be necessary for him to find a substitute response such as a suit raise on less than four-card support.
	1♠	2♡	2♠	
	1♡	1♠	Dbl	A double of a suit intervention is for business, by inference showing lack of support for opener's suit.

W.	N.	E.	S.
	1♡	1 NT	?

Responses after a 1 N.T. intervention (a strong bid) are natural and based on common sense. Generally, if North can open and East has at least 15 pts. for a no-trump bid, there's not much left for South!

5. Bidding Over Opponent's Take-Out Double:

W.	N.	E.	S.

1♡   Dbl   1♠   A simple take-out into a new suit is a rescue bid (non-forcing) showing a long—probably six-card—suit and a lack of fit for opener's suit.

1◇   Dbl   1 NT   Show 7-8 pts. and may be used as an alternative to a pass, in the hope of making West's bid difficult.

1♠   Dbl   Re-Dbl   Shows a minimum of 9 pts., no particular fit for partner's suit, and a probable interest in doubling the opponent's final contract. It guarantees the ability to make one further bid. Opener should rebid on a hand quite unfitted for defence, but otherwise pass to give South the chance for which he has asked.

1◇   Dbl   2♠   A jump bid in a new suit is a one-round force (*not* a game force) showing a good playable suit.

1♠   Dbl   2♠ or 3♠   The limit bids, when used after a take-out double are geared down in value for their pre-emptive effect.

1♡   Dbl   2 NT   A responding hand containing full values for a limit raise to the three-level (in any suit, major or minor) is shown by a conventional bid of 2 N.T. which opener should treat as he would a normal suit limit bid of three.

6. Responding to Partner's Take-Out Double:

W.	N.	E.	S.

1♠   Dbl   2◇   2♡   A bid by East lets South off the hook of replying to North's double and any bid he makes, therefore, becomes 'positive'. As North is asking for South's best suit, South

W.	N.	E.	S.	
				should always try to show a five-card suit, even on a weak hand, if he can do so at an economical level. Failing any action other than a pass by East, South should
1♡	Dbl	—	1♠	show his best suit, BUT a 'Herbert' negative, i.e. a bid of the next higher-ranking
1◇	Dbl	—	1♠	suit may be used to show a 'bust', any other bid showing at least a biddable suit. South should show a four-card major in preference to a five-card minor if the former does not involve the negative bid.
1♡	Dbl	—	1 NT	South shows a better-than-minimum hand with some hold on the suit opened.
1◇	Dbl	—	2♡	A jump response shows a good playable suit, invitational but not forcing.
1♡	Dbl	—	—	Obviously shows strength in the enemy suit and the expectation that defending the doubled contract will yield the best result.
1♣	Dbl	—	2♣	If in doubt as to the best final denomination, a cue bid of the suit opened passes the buck back to North to choose the suit. This is 'forcing to suit agreement', so on a strong hand it would be up to either member of the partnership to see that a game contract is reached.
1◇	Dbl	—	2 NT	This is a common sense bid showing a good hand with a sure hold on the suit opened.

7. Directional Asking Bids:

N.	E.	S.	W.	
1◇	1♠	2♣	—	This is a bid in the opponent's suit, which
2♠				may be used by either member of the partnership when no forcing situation
1♡	—	2♣	2◇	exists, with a view to investigating for the
3♣	—	3◇		best game contract, the accent being on the fact that this may well be 3 N.T. In each of these sequences the last bid is a D.A.B. It asks partner to clarify his hand, giving priority to a rebid in no-trumps at either the two or three-level according to strength or situation, if his hand contains

N.	E.	S.	W.
1♡	1♠	2♠	—

a partial guard in the enemy's suit, which will boost the D.A.B. bidder's own holding in the suit into at least one stop. An immediate overcall in the suit opened may be either a D.A.B. or a strong bid inferentially agreeing partner's suit as trumps. Opener should give priority to a rebid in no-trumps at either the two or three level, according to his values. If South removes into North's original suit at his next turn, it becomes clear that a no-trump contract

N.	E.	S.	W.
1♡	1♠	2♠	—
2 NT	—	3♡	—

was not his final aim, and that he was making a forcing bid with a suit fit for opener and control of the enemy's suit.

8. *Unusual No-Trump:*

W.	N.	E.	S.
1♠	No	2◇	2 NT
1♡	—	—	2 NT

Any bid in no-trumps which is clearly neither natural nor 'Blackwood' requests partner to take action with a view to a probable sacrifice contract. If two suits have been bid by the opponents, it requests partner's choice between the remaining two. If only one major has been

W.	N.	E.	S.
1♡	—	1♠	—
3♠	—	4♡	4 NT

bid, it requests his choice between the minors.

Section 6

CONTESTED AUCTIONS

Exercises

In this final section you can expect your opponents to enter the auction, either opening before your side has a chance to bid, or intervening, though in a few cases an uninterrupted sequence will also be shown to underline the difference this may make to the correct bid.

It would not be possible to cover the entire range of competitive situations in thirty examples, but at least these should give you an idea of how to cope with opposition bidding. In each case you are South, and must find your bid in the sequence shown.

No. 1   Love All, dealer East:

♠ K 4 3   E.   S.   W.   N.   E.   S.   W.   N.
♡ A 6 3   a) No   ?   b) 1 ♡   ?
♢ Q 9 5 4
♣ A 8 5

Answers: (a) If using a weak no-trump, open 1 N.T., but if that is impossible because of the range you are using, you will have to fall back on a 'prepared' 1♣.

(b) As an overcaller your hand is not strong enough for any competitive action. Pass and await developments—if any.

(Bids: 1 N.T. or 1♣ and No Bid.)

No. 2   Game All, dealer East:

♠ A 9 4   E.   S.   W.   N.   E.   S.   W.   N.
♡ K J 6 5 3 2   a) No   ?   b) 1 ♢   ?
♢ 7
♣ 6 3 2

Answers: (a) This hand, particularly being vulnerable, is not even worth an Acol light opener, so pass initially.

(b) Now you have a sensible intervening overcall, particularly as this can be made at the one-level, which needs an awful lot of defeating if the opponents are to gain a worthwhile penalty.

When you are considering making an intervening call, playing tricks are of great importance. Notice, therefore, that some hands can be worth an opening bid but not an intervening bid, whilst others can be worth an intervention but not an opening.

(Bids: No Bid and 1 ♡.)

No. 3   Game All, dealer North:

♠ 10 9   N.   E.   S.   W.   N.   E.   S.   W.
♡ K J 3   a) No 1♣   ?   b) No 1♢   ?
♢ A Q 9 8 5
♣ J 10 8   c) 1♠ 2♢   ?

Answers: (a) Being vulnerable, and particularly when partner has shown he has not got the values for an opening bid, this would be a very dangerous hand for intervention. Pass—you can always come in later if expedient.

(b) A double would be for a take-out—the last thing you want. Pass and await developments.

(c) Double ! A perfect example of the reason why it is dangerous to make an intervening overcall without adequate playing strength.

(Bids : No Bid, No Bid, and Double.)

No. 4   Love All, dealer West:

♠ Q 10 7   W.   N.   E.   S.   W.   N.   E.   S.
♡ A J 10 6   a) 1♢ No No   ?   b) No 1♠ 2♢   ?
♢ 9 6 3
♣ J 9 5

Answers: (a) Once opener's partner, East, has passed, he is known to be woefully weak, which means that there is a reasonable chance that North holds a share of the remaining goodies—perhaps a hand such as No. 1, as he could not intervene. It is, therefore, up to a player in South's position to 'protect' his partner's pass, which he may do on much lesser values than he needs in the immediate overcalling position. The weakest and, therefore, least encouraging protective bid is a change-of-suit at the one level, so here South should re-open with 1♡.

(b) Without the intervening bid South would doubtless bid 1 N.T., but he can't show a diamond guard, let alone bid at the two-level. Nor, in all decency, can he pass and the best thing he can do, even without four-card spade support, is to give partner 2♠.

(Bids : 1♡ and 2♠.)

No. 5 Game All, dealer East:

♠ K 10 8 6 E. S. W. N. E. S. W. N.
♡ A Q 9 6 3 a) 1◇ ? b) 1NT* ?
◇ A 7 2 *12-14 pts.
♣ 4

Answers : (a) You have no way of guessing whether North has a biddable major or possibly a string of clubs. *Ask* him by making a take-out double. If he bids 2♣ you can then take out into 2♡ but he will show a major suit if he can, knowing that your double implies willingness to play in either. (But compare Nos. 21, 22, and 23, which you will come to later.)

(b) You must have some method of defence against that damaging weapon, the weak no-trump, and one of the best is 'Sharples'. Here you would bid a 'Sharples' 2◇ showing a hand unsuitable for a double, which is intended primarily for penalties. 2◇ pinpoints a void or singleton club, and 2♣ would show any other hand too good to pass without a competitive effort, and on which you don't fancy a double. The convention can be used against any strength of no-trump opening though, of course, allowance must be made if the opening 1 N.T. is of the strong variety.

(Bids : Double and 2◇.)

No. 6 Love All, dealer West:

♠ A Q 10 9 6 2 W. N. E. S. W. N. E. S.
♡ K J 8 a) No No 1◇ ? b) 1◇ No No ?
◇ A 8 4
♣ 6

Answers : (a) This is a good strong single-suited hand too strong for a simple overcall (cf. No. 2b). Bid 2♠, strong and highly invitational but not forcing. It will, however, tell North that you have a hand on which you'd like to go places but want to play in spades.

(b) Now in the 'protective' position you are again much too strong for a mere 1♠ bid (cf. No. 4a)—an Acol player never tells his partner he has one sort of hand when he has, in fact, another ! Bid 2♠ which will encourage North to take action to help you if he can.

(Bids : 2♠ in both cases.)

No. 7   Game All, dealer North:

♠ Q 9 3   N.   E.   S.   W.   N.   E.   S.   W.
♡ K 10 6 4   a) 1♠ No   ?   b) 1♡   2◇   ?
◇ 8
♣ K 10 7 5 2   c) 1♠   2◇   ?

Answers: (a) There is no competitive situation and, therefore, nothing to interfere with South's natural response of 2♣.

(b) An intervening bid makes no difference at all if a responding hand can still make a natural suit limit bid. Here, without East's 2◇, South would bid 3♡, and he should do so now.

(c) When East's 2◇ bid deprives South of the two-level for the response he made in (a), it is out of the question for him to show his clubs at the three-level, and nor can he bid 2 N.T. which would show 10-12 pts. *and* a stop in diamonds. The only sensible alternative is to raise 1♠ to 2♠, even without four-card support.

(Bids : 2♣, 3♡, and 2♠.)

No. 8   Game to N-S, dealer West:

♠ K J 10 5   W.   N.   E.   S.   W.   N.   E.   S.
♡ A 10 9 6   a) No No 1◇   ?   b) 1◇ No No   ?
◇ A 8
♣ J 10 6

Answers: (a) Another hand on which you can't allow 1◇ to go uncontested, yet would prefer to *ask* your partner rather than *tell* him which suit would fit his hand best for trumps, which you do by making a take-out double. Note that partner may decide to convert this to a business double by passing, for which reason you should not double on a hand which would be disastrous for defence.

(b) In the 'protective' position the situation is different. Partner may have passed on a hand something like No. 3 and be longing for a chance to defend ! A double in the protective position shows a minimum of 12 pts. with tolerance for any suit into which partner may take out *and* a hand which you would not fear to use in defence if North decides to pass. It's the correct bid here.

(Bids : Double in both cases.)

No. 9   Game All, dealer West:

♠ K J 10 3   W. N. E. S.   W. N. E. S.
♡ A Q   a) No No 1♡ ?   b) 1♡ No No ?
◇ K 10 9
♣ K J 9 4

Answers: (a) Irrespective of the agreed value of your opening no-trump, in Acol an intervening 1 N.T. is *always strong*—a minimum of a good 15 pts. including at least two sure stops in the suit opened. Here, therefore, 1 N.T. is the perfect bid. Partner should treat it as he would a strong no-trump opening, except that 2♣ would be a weak take-out and not a fit-finding bid.

(b) 1 N.T. in the 'protective' position shows 11-15 pts. and a stop in the suit opened. Clearly South can't tell his partner that *all* he has is 11-15 pts., and a double, would do less than justice to this hand. The answer is to cue-bid the suit opened, asking partner to show his own best suit. This is 'forcing to suit agreement' which means that once a suit fit has been discovered the auction can be dropped. This in turn means that the bid can be used on quite a modest hand if of suitable shape, but that it is up to both North and South to bid up if it appears that game strength may be held.

(Bids: 1 N.T. and 2♡.)

No. 10   Game to E-W, dealer East:

♠ A K Q 9 7 4 2   E. S. W. N.   E. S. W. N.
♡ K 6   a) 1♡ ?   b) 1NT* ?
◇ A   *12-14 pts.
♣ K Q 7

Answers: (a) You can't risk doubling for a take-out and a bid of 2♠ (cf. No. 6) would not do justice to this hand. Cue-bid the suit opened against you, i.e. bid 2♡, to which partner should respond as to a take-out double. You can then bid *and rebid* spades, to show the single-suited character of your hand.

(b) Double, which you hope and expect partner will pass for penalties. Many players, on most occasions successfully, use a weak no-trump at any score, but this is going to be a moment when East will wish he hadn't! His opening bid is pretty certain to contain the two missing aces so the best you could gain as declarer would be a non-vulnerable game and the penalty is going to be a good deal more valuable.

(Bids: 2♡ and Double.)

No. 11   Love All, dealer North:

♠ Q J 9 8 5 3   N. E. S. W.   N. E. S. W.
♡ 6 3 2   a) 1◇ No ?   b) 1◇ Dbl ?
◇ 10 8
♣ 8 3

Answers : (a) There is always a temptation to show a six-card suit, particularly if it is a major, but any change-of-suit response is a one-round force, and you have not got enough to show North the values for a bid. Pass and await developments—you can always come in later, if expedient.

(b) A change-of-suit response after a take-out double is *no longer forcing*. Indeed it is a rescue operation showing a five or six-card suit which you think likely to be a better proposition than the suit partner has bid, so here you can bid 1♠. It won't deceive North, who will know that you have excellent alternative ways of showing different types of hands.

(Bids : No Bid and 1♠.)

No. 12   Love All, dealer North:

♠ 9 3   N. E. S. W.   N. E. S. W.
♡ A J 9 4   a) 1♠ 2◇ ?   b) 1♡ 2◇ ?
◇ K J 7
♣ Q 10 8 5   c) 1♠ Dbl ?

Answers: (a) The obvious bid is 2 N.T., showing the 10-12 pts. it would show without the intervening bid but, in this case, confirming the diamond guard as well.

(b) The intervening bid makes no difference at all on occasions when the responding hand is suitable for a suit limit bid. Without the 2◇ bid you would respond 3♡—do the same now.

(c) It can make a vast difference when the intervention is a take-out double. In this case, without much in partner's suit the correct bid is a redouble. The message of this is that the hand contains a minimum of 9 pts. It also guarantees the ability to make a further bid which will very likely be to double the enemy's final contract. For this reason North, unless he has an obviously more sensible course of action, should pass at his next turn to give South the chance he has asked for.

(Bids : 2 N.T., 3♡, and Redouble.)

No. 13   Love All, dealer North:

♠ Q 10 9   N.   E.   S.   W.   N.   E.   S.   W.
♡ A 9 5 2   a) 1♣   1♡   ?   b) 1♣   Dbl   ?
◇ J 7 6
♣ J 8 5

Answers :   (a) A response of 1 N.T. when the opening bid has been 1♣ shows 8-10 pts., and when there has been a suit intervening bid it also, of course, shows a guard in that suit. This hand meets these requirements, so 1 N.T. let it be.

(b) Although the correct bid in this case is also 1 N.T., it is for quite a different reason. You will remember that a change-of-suit (cf. No. 11) is a rescue bid and redouble (cf. No. 12) shows a minimum of 9 pts., so neither bid can be used here. 1 N.T. after a take-out double shows a minimum of 7 pts. though not enough for a redouble. Your possible alternative of a pass will not interfere in any way with West's reply to the double, which 1 N.T. may do.

(Bids : 1 N.T. in both cases.)

No. 14   Love All, dealer North:

♠ K Q J 9 8 6   N.   E.   S.   W.   N.   E.   S.   W.
♡ 9 5   a) 1◇   1♡   ?   b) 1◇   Dbl   ?
◇ 8 7 4
♣ A 5

Answers :   (a) The obvious bid is the one-round force of 1♠. This is so elementary that you will realise it has only been included to emphasise the difference when East, instead of passing or bidding a suit, doubles.

(b) Your hand is far too good for a 'rescue' bid of 1♠ (cf. No. 11) which would actually be asking North to pass. Nor can you redouble which, as you know, implies willingness to defend, for which your holding is quite unsuitable in spite of its count.

Make a jump bid of 2♠ which, in this situation, is a one-round force, not a game force. It will tell North of the single-suited character of your hand, which should leave him in a good position to judge whether to go on for a game or not.

(Bids : 1♠ and 2♠.)

No. 15   Game to E-W, dealer North:

♠ 9 5 3

♡ Q 10 7 4

◇ Q 8 4

♣ 10 9 8

N.	E.	S.	W.		N.	E.	S.	W.
a) 1♡	No	?		b) 1♡	Dbl	?	

Answers: (a) Whether or not East makes a bid you haven't enough to show support for partner, so pass. The best you can say about your hand is that at least it contains four-card heart support!

(b) Once more the double makes a difference, and this time you should raise to 2♡. You will realise that this ranks as a limit bid, but that the limit is very much lower than in an uninterrupted sequence. The idea, of course, is to make things as difficult as possible for West, who has not yet had a chance to reply to his partner's question about his best suit.

(Bids : No Bid and 2♡.)

No. 16   Game All, dealer North:

♠ K J 2

♡ J 10 8 5 4

◇ 9 6 2

♣ 8 5

N.	E.	S.	W.		N.	E.	S.	W.
a) 1♡	No	?		b) 1♡	Dbl	?	

Answers: (a) Vulnerable particularly, you haven't enough 'shape' to do more than give a single raise to 2♡ on this hand.

(b) The double again makes a difference and here, on the same principle that made you give a single raise on No. 15 with less than the standard requirements for the bid, you should bid 3♡. This will have the maximum possible pre-emptive effect on West, who has yet to bid. He *may* be able to bid 3♠, but either minor will have to be shown at the four-level. In any case, with the double on your right, your ♠K-J are likely to be well placed.

(Bids : 2♡ and 3♡.)

No. 17   Game All, dealer North:

♠ 10 9
♡ K 10 7 4
◇ A 8 4 2
♣ K 6 4

	N.	E.	S.	W.		N.	E.	S.	W.
a)	1♡	No	?		b)	1♡	Dbl	?	

Answers: (a) It wouldn't matter whether East passed or made a suit intervening bid here, as this makes no difference to your response when you have a suit limit bid available. The correct and accurate bid here is 3♡.

(b) You have already learned (No. 16) that, following a take-out double, a raise to the three-level is used purely pre-emptively, from which it follows that, in this situation, another bid must be found when a responding hand contains a genuine three-level limit bid. The answer is to use a *conventional* bid of 2 N.T. (an otherwise idle bid, as these values would be shown by a redouble) which shows the full values for a normal limit bid at the three-level. North will treat this as he would the 3♡ bid in (a) above, simply signing-off by converting to 3♡, bidding 4♡ if he would have done so in reply to 3♡, or taking any stronger action he thinks justified.

(Bids : 3♡ and 2 N.T.)

No. 18   Game All, dealer South:

♠ A J 10 9 7
♡ 9 5
◇ 7
♣ K Q 10 8 2

	S.	W.	N.	E.		S.	W.	N.	E.
a)	1♣	Dbl	Redbl	1◇	b)	1♣	Dbl	Redbl	No
	?					?			

Answers: (a) As long as you fully understand what North means when he bids over West's take-out double, you won't find much difficulty in adjusting your own rebids accordingly. In this sequence North has shown a minimum of 9 honour points and a probable willingness to double, and then defend, the opponents' final contract. The last thing you want to do on this weak two-suiter is to defend, so warn North of this immediately by rebidding 1♠ instead of allowing the bidding to run round to him for action.

(b) This makes no difference to the fact that you don't want to defend. North's redouble let East off the hook of replying to his partner's double but it doesn't change your view. Tell North this by bidding 1♠.

(Bids : 1♠ in either case.)

No. 19   Game All, dealer South:

♠ 9 5 3   S.   W.   N.   E.   S.   W.   N.   E.
♡ A K J 10 9 4   a) 1♡ Dbl 1♠ No   b) 1♡ Dbl Redbl 2◇
◇ 7 6   ?   ?
♣ K 10

Answers : (a) Check back to No. 11 if you've forgotten the type
of hand your partner, North, is likely to have. Pass and leave it to
him—he's lucky to be finding three spades in your hand if he
becomes declarer.

(b) This is essentially the same situation as in No. 18—you have
no interest in defence even if North has the values for a redouble.
Tell him this by taking out into 2♡.

(Bids : No Bid and 2♡.)

No. 20   Game All, dealer South:

♠ A 10 9   S.   W.   N.   E.   S.   W.   N.   E.
♡ K J 10 7   a) 1♡ Dbl 1♠ No   b) 1♡ Dbl Redbl No
◇ K J 10   ?   ?
♣ A J 9

Answers: (a) Without West's double, North's 1♠ would have
been a one-round force to which you would have rebid 2 N.T. Now,
however, that you know he is making a weak rescue bid, it would be
foolish indeed to go to this high level. Bid 1 N.T. which North, in
turn, should recognise as showing the values for a 2 N.T. bid in an
uninterrupted sequence. If North takes out into 2♠, you will pass.

(b) You are only too happy to allow North to take the next
action, and if this is to double any get-out attempt by West, it will
suit you excellently to defend. With 17 honour points in your hand
and North's minimum of 9 pts. you have a combined total of at
least 26 pts., which must unstitch the vulnerable East-West in no
uncertain terms. So pass and await developments.

(Bids : 1 N.T. and No Bid.)

No. 21   Game All, dealer West:

♠ 8 6 3
♡ Q 10 9 4
◇ 8 5 4
♣ 9 3 2

W.	N.	E.	S.		W.	N.	E.	S.
a) 1♣	Dbl	No	?	b)	1♡	Dbl	No	?

Answers :   (a) On very weak hands such as this, where the bidding level must be kept as low as possible, many players find it convenient to use some sort of negative or 'bust' response. Recently I have been using a 'Herbert' negative, that is, a bid of the next higher ranking suit to show not even a four-card suit which can be bid at the one level. This has proved very satisfactory and, using it, you would bid 1♡ here. North will know that it is at least a four-card suit because you did not use the 'bust' response of 1◇.

(b) This time it is your only four-card suit which has been doubled, so you respond 1♠.

An important point to remember is that if East bids over the double, this lets South off the hook of responding and any bid he makes is, therefore, 'positive', showing at least a four-card suit. But South should always try to help his partner by showing his best suit as long as this can be at the one-level so in (a), had East bid 1◇, South should still bid 1♡, but had East bid 1♡ or 1♠, South should pass.

(Bids : 1♡ and 1♠.)

No. 22   Game All, dealer West:

♠ 10 3
♡ Q J 10 9 4 3
◇ 7 6
♣ K 9 2

W.	N.	E.	S.		W.	N.	E.	S.
a) 1♣	Dbl	1◇	?	b)	1♠	Dbl	No	?

Answers :   (a) Whether East bids his 1◇ or not, the answer would be the same here—South must make it clear to North that he is not showing a hand such as No. 21 above. Make a jump bid of 2♡, showing a genuinely playable suit.

(b) It would be cramping the auction to jump to 3♡ here so bid 2♡. But North will know that you did not use the negative bid of 2♣ and that you did not fear to raise the level of the bidding to show your suit.

(Bids : 2♡ in either case.)

No. 23   Game All, dealer West:

♠ J 9 7 6   W.   N.   E.   S.   W.   N.   E.   S.
♡ Q 10 8 4   a) 1♢ Dbl No   ?   b) 1♡ Dbl No   ?
♢ 9 5 4
♣ K 7

Answers : (a) If you are using a Herbert negative you are prevented from using your simplest answer of 1♡ but, as almost
always happens, your hand contains an alternative, in this instance
1♠. North will notice that you did not use a negative response,
even if 1♠ isn't very encouraging!

(b) This time the 'bust' response would be 1♠, which you would
like to avoid, but you have no sensible alternative.

(Bids: 1♠ and 1♠.)

No. 24   Game All, dealer West:

♠ K 10 9 8   W.   N.   E.   S.   W.   N.   E.   S.
♡ A J 9 3   a) 1♣ Dbl No   ?   b) 1♡ Dbl No   ?
♢ 9 5 4
♣ K 8

Answers : (a) On a promising hand, and particularly when you
are doubtful as to the best final denomination, cue-bid the suit
opened against you, so here bid 2♣. This bid is what is known as
'forcing to suit agreement'—in other words, the bidding can be
dropped below game level once the best suit fit has been discovered,
so it is up to either of the partnership to bid strongly if he thinks a
game contract should be reached. This cue bid is, of course, a
'passing the buck' bid, and if North next bids 2♢ South should
pass. If North bids either 2♡ or 2♠, South should raise to three
and leave the rest to North.

(b) When 1♡ is doubled a cue bid of 2♡ would not be sensible.
Nor would an apparent negative of 1♠ or a jump to 2♠ on a
four-card suit. Bid 2 N.T. showing the excellent count and hold on
the enemy suit.

(Bids : 2♣ and 2 N.T.)

No. 25   Game to E-W, dealer South:

♠ K J 7
♡ Q 5
◇ A K 10 9 8
♣ A J 8

S.	W.	N.	E.		S.	W.	N.	E.
a) 1◇	No	1♡	1♠	b)	1◇	No	2♣	2♡
?					?			

Answers : (a) With 18 pts. and an excellent guard in the suit bid
on your right you have no problems. Bid the obvious 2 N.T. This
question was only included to pinpoint the difference when, though
you suspect that a final no-trump contract would be the best, your
own stop in the enemy suit is flimsy.

(b) With only ♡Q-x it would be pure 'shooting' to bid in no-
trumps at this stage. *Ask* your partner if he can help to boost your
own partial heart stop by making a Directional Asking Bid (D.A.B.)
of 3♡. North will give priority to a rebid of 3 N.T. if he can help
to stop the suit. If he can't, he will make the most sensible rebid
available and you will know that your ♡Q-x isn't going to be
enough to make 3 N.T. a good contract.

(Bids : 2 N.T. and 3♡.)

No. 26   Game All, dealer South:

♠ A J 8
♡ Q 6
◇ K Q J 8 3
♣ A 9 8

S.	W.	N.	E.		S.	W.	N.	E.
a) 1◇	1♠	2♣	No	b)	1◇	No	1♡	2♣
?					?			

Answers : (a) With 17 pts. and a good stop in West's spades,
again the best rebid is 2 N.T. It's true that you have only ♡Q-x, an
unbid suit, but North has responded at the two-level without his own
ace, and it's odds-on that he will have something in hearts.

(b) Here South has a guard in the clubs bid by East, but it is very
possible that if a final contract of 3 N.T. can be placed with declarer
as North, it will be safer. If, for example, North holds ♣Q-x, a club
lead from East would turn this into a double stop or, alternatively,
the defence would have to give up a defensive tempo by attacking
in another suit. So again, instead of just bidding 3 N.T., make a
Directional Asking Bid of 3♣ in the hope that North can bid 3 N.T.

(Bids : 2 N.T. and 3♣.)

No. 27   Love All, dealer North:

♠ 8 6
♡ Q 9 7
♢ A 10 7 6 4
♣ Q 5 2

N.	E.	S.	W.		N.	E.	S.	W.
a) 1♣	No	1♢	1♡	b) 1♣	No	1♢	1♠
2♡	No	?		2♠	No	?	

Answers : (a) North has made a Directional Asking Bid enquiring whether South has a partial heart stop which will help to 'boost' his own heart holding, with a view to a final contract of 3 N.T. South can do this, so should give priority to a response in no-trumps. In this case he is only strong enough to bid 2 N.T., but note that, if he had a stronger hand, it would be up to him to bid 3 N.T., not a mere 2 N.T. which would leave the onus on North.

(b) Again North has made a Directional Asking Bid, though this time in spades, a suit in which South can do nothing to help. He must, therefore, make the most sensible rebid his hand suggests, in this case 3♣.

(Bids : 2 N.T. and 3♣.)

No. 28   Game to E-W, dealer West:

♠ 9
♡ 10
♢ QJ854
♣ KJ5432

W.	N.	E.	S.		W.	N.	E.	S.
a) 1♡	No	1♠	?	b) 1♠	No	3♠	?

Answers : (a) Here we come to the use of the Unusual No Trump, which simply means a bid in no-trumps in a situation where it really cannot show a genuine wish to play in that denomination. If South bids 1 N.T. at this point, it would show a strong hand with stops in both majors. What he has in mind, however, is a possible sacrifice in clubs or diamonds, so he bids 2 N.T. asking for North's preference between the *two unbid suits*. A further bid by West would let North off the hook of responding to this bid, though he may well be able to judge that a sacrifice contract of 5♣ or 5♢ would be worth while, even if doubled.

(b) In this sequence only one major suit has been bid by East-West and South, by bidding 3 N.T., could not possibly be showing a wish to play in that contract. He is asking, not for North's choice between the three unbid suits, but for his choice between the *minors*.

(Bids : 2 N.T. and 3 N.T.)

No. 29   Game to N-S, dealer West:

♠ K 10 9 2
♡ 8 3
♢ K J 7 6
♣ A Q 6

	W.	N.	E.	S.		W.	N.	E.	S.
a)	3♡	3♠	No	4♣	b)	3♡	3♠	No	4♣
	No	4 NT	—	?		No	4 NT	5♡	?

Answers: (a) This is easy—the response to a 'Blackwood' 4 N.T. when you hold one ace is 5♢, so that's the correct bid here.

(b) Doubtless East passed on the first round seeing no need to interfere until he saw that North-South were trying for a slam. At this point he came to life and bid 5♡, preparing for a sacrifice, and also interfering with South's normal response to his partner's 'Blackwood' 4 N.T. In these circumstances the responses are modified, a pass showing no ace, five of the next higher ranking suit one ace, and so on. So here South should bid 5♠.

(Bids: 5♢ and 5♠.)

No. 30   Game to N-S, dealer West:

♠ A K J 8 6 3
♡ A
♢ A Q 10 9 7 2
♣ —

	W.	N.	E.	S.		W.	N.	E.	S.
a)	No	No	1♡	2♡	b)	No	No	1 NT*	?
	No	3♣	No	?		*12-14 pts.			

Answers: (a) The initial 2♡ cue-bid showed a powerful hand unsuitable for a take-out double, to which North has responded, not unexpectedly, with 3♣. The 2♡ bid is forcing to game. So North should show 4-card suits in *ascending* order until game has been reached.

(b) South doesn't want to defend on this hand which makes it impossible for him to double. The correct bid is the Acol conventional 2 N.T., showing a powerful two-suiter. This is forcing to game, and North must reply as he would to a take-out double. Thereafter South will have a chance to show both suits and North will steer the contract into the one which fits his hand best.

(Bids: 3♡ and 2 N.T.)

Section 6
CONTESTED AUCTIONS
Competition Quiz

♠♡♣◇♠♡♣◇♠♡♣◇♠♡♣◇♠♡♣◇♠♡♣◇♠♡♣◇♠♡♣◇♠♡♣◇

In competition against another player, one should answer the three questions in the **A** set, and the other the three questions in the **B** set on each page. In each case the dealer is the first-named player in the auction, and South's bid—or next bid—in the relative sequence is required. The score, unless otherwise stated, is Love All.

1A.

1. ♠ Q 7 4	2. ♠ K J 7 6 3	3. ♠ K 7 6
♡ K J 9 6 3	♡ 8 5 2	♡ Q 6 5
◇ 10 8 6	◇ A 7	◇ A 9 7 3
♣ 6 4	♣ Q 6 3	♣ A 6 2

N. E. S. W.	W. N. E. S.	N. E. S. W.
1♡ 2♣ ?	No 1◇ 1♡ ?	No 1◇ ?

Answers: Bid (2 pts.) Reason (3 pts.)

1. 2♡ Provided a responding hand is suitable for a limit bid, an intervening bid makes no difference at all.

2. 1♠ Nothing about East's 1♡ intervention has interfered with your natural response of 1♠.

3. No As opener you would doubtless have bid 1 N.T. (weak)
   Bid but you have no playing strength. Pass and bid later if expedient.

1B.

1. ♠ A 7	2. ♠ 9 5	3. ♠ A 9 4
♡ K J 6 5 3	♡ Q 8 6	♡ 7 6
◇ 9 7 4	◇ J 10 7	◇ Q 7 2
♣ Q 6 3	♣ K J 7 4 2	♣ K J 9 8 3

N. E. S. W.	N. E. S. W.	N. E. S. W.
No 1♠ ?	1♡ 2◇ ?	1♡ 2♣ ?

Answers: Bid (2 pts.) Reason (3 pts.)

1. No This hand is very similar to No. 2 above, but this time
   Bid you would be forced into bidding at the two-level—highly dangerous without better playing strength.

2. 2♡ This hand is not strong enough to show the clubs at the three-level so, in spite of the lack of four-card heart support, it is wiser to give a simple raise in hearts.

3. Dbl Just the sort of hand that makes it so dangerous to intervene at the two-level without adequate playing strength.

2A.

1.	♠ A 9 8	2.	♠ 7 2	3.	♠ K 10 5 4
	♡ J 9 6 4		♡ K J 10 8 5		♡ K J 9 6
	◇ A 6 3		◇ A Q 6		◇ A 7 4
	♣ Q 8 5		♣ 8 5 3		♣ 8 6

W.	N.	E.	S.		N.	E.	S.	W.		N.	E.	S.	W.
1♡	No	No	?		1♣	2♡	?			1♣	2♡	?	

Answers:

Bid (2 pts.)   Reason (3 pts.)

1. 1 N.T. Comparing this with **1A**, No. 3 you might think you should pass, but this time you are in the 'protective' position, where 1 N.T. shows 11-15 pts. with a guard in the suit opened. Quite different values are needed for re-opening the bidding after two passes.

2. Dbl. With such poor support for North's spades, this is the most probable way of gaining a plus score on the deal.

3. 3♠ Without the intervening 2♡ you would have raised to 3♠ and should do so now. Your spade support is too good to expect this suit to yield a comfortable number of tricks in defence.

2B.

1.	♠ K J 10 3	2.	♠ A J 9 3	3.	♠ 9 4
	♡ A 9 2		♡ K 10 8		♡ 8 6
	◇ Q J 6		◇ A J 6		◇ J 10 9
	♣ A J 7		♣ 9 6 5		♣ Q 10 9 8 5 3

E.	S.	W.	N.		W.	N.	E.	S.		W.	N.	E.	S.
1♠	?				1◇	No	No	?		1♡	1NT	No	?

Answers:

Bid (2 pts.)   Reason (3 pts.)

1. 1 N.T. Used as an overcall, 1 N.T. is *always strong*, irrespective of the agreed strength of the opening no-trump. It shows a minimum of 15, if not more, pts. with a double guard in the suit bid.

2. Dbl. In the protective position you should double on a hand of 9 or more pts. on which you would also be happy to defend if partner converts to a business double by passing. Note that the hand is not suitable for a protective 1 N.T. or a cue bid of 2◇.

3. 2♣ South should treat North's 1 N.T. overcall as he would a strong no-trump opening except that 2♣ is a natural weak take-out and not a fit-finding bid unless Stayman is used in this situation by agreement.

3A.

1. ♠ A J 9 3
   ♡ K 10 8
   ◇ A J 6
   ♣ 9 6 5
   E. S. W. N.
   1♣ ?

2. ♠ K 7 3
   ♡ K Q 8 5 4
   ◇ Q 7
   ♣ 9 6 2
   W. N. E. S.
   1◇ No No ?

3. ♠ K 7
   ♡ A K J 7 6 5
   ◇ 9 6 3
   ♣ 8 4
   W. N. E. S.
   No No 1♣ ?

Answers:

Bid (2 pts.)   Reason (3 pts.)

1. No   This is the same hand as **2B**. No 2 and in this position
   Bid   there is no sensible bid to make.. Pass—your main
          hope is that West will also pass and North will be able
          to make a 'protective' double, which you would pass
          happily.

2. 1♡   You should generally re-open the bidding on as little
          as 9 pts. if you can do this at the one-level. Here South
          has 10 pts. and can bid 1♡ without fear of misleading
          North.

3. 2♡   The ♠K is well-placed over the opening bid, and the
          excellent six-card suit in addition makes this hand well
          worth an attempt at competition.

3B.

1. ♠ A 6
   ♡ A K J 7 6 5
   ◇ K 10 9
   ♣ 9 2
   W. N. E. S.
   No No 1♣ ?

2. ♠ K 7 3
   ♡ K Q J 8 5 4
   ◇ 9 6
   ♣ A 5
   W. N. E. S.
   1◇ No No ?

3. ♠ K J 9 2
   ♡ A J 7 4
   ◇ 10
   ♣ A J 6 3
   W. N. E. S.
   1◇ No No ?

Answers:

Bid (2 pts.)   Reason (3 pts.)

1. 3♡   You can't leave North to think you have nothing better
          than Hand No. 3 at the top of this page. Jump cne
          step, strong and invitational but not forcing.

2. 2♡   This time you can't let North think you have only a
          modest little collection like No. 2 above. Jump one step
          to show the excellent suit plus outside values.

3. 2◇   Not a hand for a 'protective' double because you don't
          want to defend if North's pass were based on good
          diamonds. Cue-bid 2◇, forcing to suit agreement, which
          means that once a suit fit has been found the auction
          can be dropped below game level. Equally it is up to
          both North and South to bid on if a game seems likely.

4A.

1. ♠ A Q 9 5	2. ♠ K Q J 8 5 4	3. ♠ A J 7 4 2
♡ K J 8 4	♡ A	♡ K J 9 5
◇ 7 3	◇ 4	◇ K J 6
♣ K J 9	♣ A K J 10 7	♣ 7

E. S. W. N.	E. S. W. N.	E. S. W. N.
1◇ ?	1◇ ?	1NT*?
		*12-14 pts.

Answers: Bid (2 pts.)   Reason (3 pts.)

1.   Dbl.   Obviously South must try to compete on this hand, but it is one on which he would like to discuss with North, rather than tell him, their best final denomination.

2.   2◇   South can't sensibly double to ask for North's choice of suit—North must be told at once that South's hand is not suitable for a double. A cue bid of the suit opened is the correct choice.

3.   2◇   Some form of defence to a no-trump opening is a 'must' for your armoury, and examples here are based on 'Sharples'. A bid of 2◇ pinpoints a void or singleton club. North should show his best suit and the contract should end in the one that fits the combined hands best.

4B.

1. ♠ Q 9 2	2. ♠ 7 3	3. ♠ K Q 8 6
♡ K Q J 9 8 5	♡ K J 5	♡ A J 10 7
◇ A 6	◇ Q 10 8 2	◇ 10
♣ K 2	♣ A J 5 4	♣ A Q 9 3

E. S. W. N.	N. E. S. W.	W. N. E. S.
1NT*?	1♠ Dbl ?	1◇ No No 2◇
*12-14 pts.		No 2♠ No ?

Answers: Bid (2 pts.)   Reason (3 pts.)

1.   Dbl.   To bid 2♡ would be craven—this is an ideal hand for a business (*not* a take-out) double. It contains a good suit in which to attack and the best chance of a good plus score will come from defence.

2.   Re-dbl.   This shows a minimum of 9 pts., no particular fit for North's suit, and a probable interest in doubling the final contract reached by E-W. It also promises the ability to make a further bid.

3.   4♠   As the 2◇ cue bid is forcing to suit agreement only, it is up to South, if he thinks the combined hands will produce a game, to bid it, and not to leave it to North.

5A.

1. ♠ K 9 7 3	2. ♠ A 9 3	3. ♠ 9 6 3
♡ J 8	♡ Q 10 7	♡ Q J 7 5 4 2
◇ J 6 2	◇ J 6 4	◇ 8
♣ 10 8 5 4	♣ 10 8 5 4	♣ 8 5 4

N. E. S. W.	N. E. S. W.	N. E. S. W.
1♣ Dbl ?	1◇ Dbl ?	1◇ Dbl ?

Answers: Bid (2 pts.)   Reason (3 pts.)

1. 2♣   Without the intervening double you would only just scrape up a single raise. After the double you may make such a bid on even less than normal values, for its pre-emptive effect.

2. 1 N.T. After an intervening double 1 N.T. is used as a pre-emptive nuisance-bid, showing 7-8 pts., or just possibly a 'bad' 9 pts., (cf. **4B**, No. 2) which are not worth a redouble.

3. 1♡   After the double a simple change-of-suit is no longer a one round force. It is purely a rescue bid warning partner of a poor fit for his suit and a playable suit of your own.

5B.

1. ♠ Q J 7 5 4 2	2. ♠ 9 3	3. ♠ K J 9 2
♡ 9 6 3	♡ K Q J 7 5 4	♡ K 10 6 4
◇ 8	◇ A 6 3	◇ A 9 2
♣ 8 5 4	♣ J 10	♣ 6 4

N. E. S. W.	N. E. S. W.	N. E. S. W.
1♡ Dbl ?	1◇ Dbl ?	1♠ Dbl ?

Answers: Bid (2 pts.)   Reason (3 pts.)

1. No   Your clue comes from No. 3 above. Had North been
    Bid doubled in 1◇ you would have rescued into 1♠. As it is, with a three-card fit, don't rescue into something which may be less good.

2. 2♡   Again your clue is in No. 3 above, as you must distinguish between a weak 'rescue operation' and a genuine bid with a good playable suit. 2♡ is a one-round force after the double, not a game force as it would be otherwise.

3. 2 N.T. Following a double both the single and double raise limit bids are used pre-emptively on reduced values. A genuine full-strength limit raise to the three-level is shown by a *conventional* response of 2 N.T.

6A.

1. ♠ K Q 10 8 6 4	2. ♠ K 8 6 5	3. ♠ K J 9
♡ J 9	♡ A J 9 2	♡ Q 9 7 4
◇ 7 2	◇ 6	◇ A 6 3
♣ A 8 5	♣ Q 10 8 4	♣ A J 7

S.	W.	N.	E.
1♠	Dbl	Re-	No
		dbl	
?			

N.	E.	S.	W.
1◇	Dbl	Re-	No
		Dbl	
No	1♡	?	

S.	W.	N.	E.
1♣	Dbl	1♠	No
?			

Answers: Bid (2 pts.)   Reason (3 pts.)

1. 2♠ By his redouble, North showed willingness to defend East-West's contract, probably doubling at his next turn. Tell him this is highly unattractive on your light opener by taking out.

2. Dbl. Your redouble showed at least 9 pts. and a probable wish to double the final East-West contract. What could be more what the doctor ordered? North has shown willingness to co-operate by his pass.

3. No   You opened 1♣ being too strong for 1 N.T. Remem-
    Bid ber the sort of hand North is showing (cf. **5A**, No. 3) and pass.

6B.

1. ♠ K 7 9	2. ♠ K Q 7 4 3	3. ♠ K Q 10 8 6 4
♡ Q 9 7 4	♡ A J 9	♡ J 9
◇ A 6 3	◇ K Q 6	◇ 7 2
♣ A J 7	♣ Q 6	♣ A 8 5

S.	W.	N.	E.
1♣	Dbl	2NT	No
?			

S.	W.	N.	E.
1♠	Dbl	Re-	No
		dbl	
?			

S.	W.	N.	E.
1♠	Dbl	2NT	No
?			

Answers: Bid (2 pts.)   Reason (3 pts.)

1. 3 N.T. Compare No. 3 above and **5B**, No. 3. If North raised 1♣ to 3♣ without the intervening double you'd try 3 N.T., and it's only common sense to try it now.

2. No   Give North the chance he has asked for, which is to
    Bid bid again. West has yet to make his self-rescue attempt, and you will be glad to defend anything North may double. If West should pass you could be in many a worse contract than this!

3. 3♠ Without the double, had North raised your 1♠ to 3♠, you would have passed. So now convert his conventional 2 N.T. to 3♠.

7A.

1. ♠ K Q 7 5 3	2. ♠ J 8 6 5 3	3. ♠ Q 10 9 4
♡ A J 6	♡ 9 2	♡ Q J 6 2
◇ A J 5 4	◇ 8 7 4	◇ K 8 4
♣ 7	♣ 9 8 7	♣ 7 6

S.	W.	N.	E.	W.	N.	E.	S.	W.	N.	E.	S.
1♠	Dbl	Re	2◇	1◇	Dbl	1♡	?	1♡	Dbl	No	?
		dbl									

?

Answer:
Bid (2pts.)   Reason (3pts.)

1. **Dbl.** North, by his original redouble, has shown a probable desire to defend East-West's final contract (doubled). Tell him that you can go along with this, and can yourself cope with the diamond suit.

2. **1♠** North, by his double, has *asked* you which suit you prefer. Help him out, never forgetting, of course, the type of hand East should have.

3. **1 N.T.** If, as I hope, you have adopted the 'Herbert negative' you don't want to bid 1♠ here. You can, however, perfectly well bid 1 N.T., showing a better-than-bust and stop in spades.

7B.

1. ♠ J 7	2. ♠ K J 7	3. ♠ J 10
♡ 8 6 5 3	♡ K J 9	♡ Q 10 8 5
◇ 9 4 2	◇ A J 6	◇ K 7 5 4 2
♣ 10 9 7 5	♣ A 7 5 4	♣ 8 4

W.	N.	E.	S.	S.	W.	N.	E.	W.	N.	E.	S.
1♡	Dbl	No	?	1♣	Dbl	1♡	1♠	1♣	Dbl	No	?
				?							

Answer:
Bid (2pts.)   Reason (3pts.)

1. **1♠** This is a true 'bust'. Bid a 'Herbert' 1♠ to warn North.

2. **2♡** Remembering the type of hand North will have, 2♡ is quite enough at this stage, *not* the 2 N.T. you would bid in an uninterrupted sequence.

3. **1♡** Apart from the fact that you should always show a major suit if you can, 1◇ would be the 'Herbert' negative, a bid you can avoid.

8A.

1.	♠ A 9 7 2	2.	♠ K J 10 7 5 3	3.	♠ Q 6
	♡ K J 10 5		♡ 9 5		♡ 8 2
	◊ 6		◊ K 6		◊ Q J 10 9 6 3
	♣ K 9 8 4		♣ J 7 4		♣ J 10 8

W.	N.	E.	S.		W.	N.	E.	S.		W.	N.	E.	S.
1◊	Dbl	No	?		1♡	Dbl	No	?		1◊	Dbl	No	?

Answers:

Bid (2 pts.)   Reason (3 pts.)

1.   2◊   Cue-bid 2◊, the suit opened—and doubled—which passes the buck back to North to make the choice.

2.   2♠   Apart from the fact that 1♠ would be negative, it is essential to distinguish, for North's sake, between a suit of this value and one such as you held in **7B**, No. 3.

3.   No   Convert North's take-out double to a business one by
     Bid   passing, surely your best chance of a good plus score on the hand.

8B.

1.	♠ K Q 9 7	2.	♠ 9 5	3.	♠ A J 9 4
	♡ K 8 5		♡ K J 10 7 5 3		♡ K J 8 3
	◊ A K 6		◊ K 6		◊ 6
	♣ K J 3		♣ J 7 4		♣ K 10 7 4

W.	N.	E.	S.		W.	N.	E.	S.		W.	N.	E.	S.
1◊	No	No	?		1♠	Dbl	No	?		1◊	Dbl	No	2◊
										No	2♡	No	?

Answers:

Bid (2 pts.)   Reason (3 pts.)

1.   2 NT   2 NT shows 19-20 balanced points. North will almost certainly take out into a suit after which you can decide whether to go for a game in his suit or in no-trumps.

2.   2♡   Comparing this with No. 2 above you might want to bid 3♡, but this will cramp the auction. Partner will not miss the fact that you did not bid a negative 2♣.

3.   4♡   As your 2◊ was forcing to suit agreement only, you could pass. On the other hand, your values facing North who could double must surely be worth a try for game.

9A.

1. ♠ K 10 8 5   2. ♠ A K 10 7 4   3. ♠ A 10 9 2
   ♡ Q 10 9   ♡ A J 8   ♡ K 9 8 4
   ◇ K 8 2   ◇ Q 6   ◇ K J 6
   ♣ 9 7 3   ♣ K J 5   ♣ J 3

N.	E.	S.	W.		S.	W.	N.	E.		N.	E.	S.	W.
1♠	2♡	2♠	No		1♠	2◇	2♡	No		1♣	1◇	1♠	No
3♣	No	?			?					2◇	No	?	

Answers: Bid (2 pts.)   Reason (3 pts.)

1   3♠   3♣ in this situation is a trial bid, just as it would be without East's 2◇ intervention. However, there's nothing to be done by South except sign off in 3♠.

2   3◇   This is a Directional Asking Bid designed to discover whether 3 N.T., 4♡, or 4♠ will be the best final contract. If North can help with a partial stop in diamonds he will give priority to a rebid in no-trumps.

3. 3 N.T. This time it is North who is making a Directional Asking Bid. With a very adequate diamond stop and 12½ pts., South should give an affirmative reply of 3 N.T., not a mere 2 N.T.

9B.

1. ♠ A K 9 7 3   2. ♠ 9   3. ♠ A J 6
   ♡ K J 7   ♡ K J 9 8 5   ♡ Q 4
   ◇ K J 6   ◇ Q 10 7 6   ◇ A Q J 6 3
   ♣ Q 4   ♣ A J 7   ♣ A 10 7

S.	W.	N.	E.		W.	N.	E.	S.		S.	W.	N.	E.
1♠	No	2◇	2♡		1♠	2♣	2♠	?		1◇	No	1♡	2♣
?										?			

Answers: Bid (2 pts.)   Reason (3 pts.)

1. 2 N.T. This shows the count and heart guard. It's true South has only ♣Q-x, but North has bid at the two-level without his own ◇K-J and he must have something!

2. 3♣   Responding to an intervening bid is different from responding to an opening bid. South's simple change-of-suit would not be forcing, so support for what must be at least a five-card suit should be shown in preference to a new suit of doubtful value.

3. 3♣   Another D.A.B. If North has as much as ♣Q-x, 3 N.T. is likely to play better from his hand than from South's. There's plenty of time to decide on the best final contract.

10A.

1. ♠ K J 7 5	2. ♠ 7 3	3. ♠ K 10 9 3
♡ A 9 6 2	♡ Q 9 2	♡ Q 8 7 4
◇ 8 2	◇ A 10 8 6 5	◇ Q 6
♣ A 10 7	♣ Q 8 3	♣ 8 4 2

E.	S.	W.	N.
1NT*?			
*12-14 pts.			

N.	E.	S.	W.
1♣	1♡	2◇	No
2♡	No	?	

N.	E.	S.	W.
No	1NT*	No	No
2♣	No	?	
*12-14 pts.			

Answers: Bid (2 pts.)   Reason (3 pts.)

1. 2♣   This bid, in the 'Sharples' defence, takes the place of a double (which would be for business) when you want to compete against a no-trump opening but are not strong enough to double. Note that 2♣ is a take-out request which is used except when there is a void or singleton club, when the bid is 2◇.

2. 2 N.T.   North's 2♡ is a Directional Asking Bid. South must confirm that he holds at least a partial guard in hearts.

3. No   When a player has previously passed (using 'Sharples')
    Bid   his 2♣ or 2◇ becomes natural and not a conventional take-out request.

10B.

1. ♠ 6	2. ♠ A 7	3. ♠ A J 8 6 3
♡ K 4	♡ K Q 10 9 6 5	♡ K J 9 2
◇ K J 9 7 2	◇ 8 3	◇ A 7
♣ A 10 9 7 3	♣ Q 6 2	♣ 3 2

E.	S.	W.	N.
1NT*	2◇	No	2♡
No	?		
*12-14 pts.			

W.	N.	E.	S.
1 NT*	2♣	No	?
*12-14 pts.			

W.	N.	E.	S.
1 NT*	2◇	No	?
*12-14 pts.			

Answers: Bid (2 pts.)   Reason (3 pts.)

1. 3♣   North will have understood 2◇ as a take-out request with a void or singleton club. Now 3♣ shows a minor two-suiter.

2. 3♡   In response to North's 'Sharples' 2♣ this hand is too good for a mere 2♡. 3♡ shows a good playable suit and is highly invitational, not forcing.

3. 2 N.T.   This conventionally passes the buck back to North to pick his own best suit. It is forcing to the four-level only, that is, to a major suit game if a fit is found.

11A.

1. ♠ K 3	2. ♠ —	3. ♠ 7 4
♡ —	♡ 5	♡ 6 2
◇ K J 7 3 2	◇ 10 8 7 6 5 3	◇ K J 6
♣ Q 10 9 6 3 2	♣ J 9 6 5 3 2	♣ A Q J 7 5 3

Game to E-W:	Game to E-W:	Game All:
W. N. E. S.	N. E. S. W.	W. N. E. S.
1♣ No 3♡ ?	No 1♠ No 3♡	1♠ 2◇ 2♡ ?
	No 4♡ ?	

Answers: Bid (2 pts.) Reason (3 pts.)

1. 3 N.T. With an apparently worthless hand in defence of what is going to be at least a vulnerable game contract, South suggests a sacrifice in one of the two unbid suits, by a bid in no-trumps when this cannot possibly show a genuine wish to play in that denomination.

2. 4 N.T. South passed initially to see whether East-West were going to reach a game contract. Now not only a game, but a slam contract seems probable and a sacrifice in one or other of the two unbid suits must surely be profitable.

3. 3◇ With adequate diamond support, raise North's suit rather than show even a six-card club suit, (cf. **9B**, No.2 on p. 194).

11B.

1. ♠ A K J 8 6 4	2. ♠ 7 6	3. ♠ Q 10 5
♡ —	♡ K J 9	♡ K 9 7 3
◇ A K J 6 5	◇ A Q 9 8 2	◇ 8
♣ K 5	♣ Q 7 5	♣ K Q 7 5 2

E. S. W. N.	N. E. S. W.	W. N. E. S.
1 NT* ?	1♣ 1♡ 2◇ No	No 1♠ 2 NT ?
*12-13 pts.	2♡ No ?	

Answers: Bid (2 pts.) Reason (3 pts.)

1. 2 N.T. Far too good for a simple take-out request and unsuitable for a double. Use the Acol conventional bid of 2 N.T., a game force showing a powerful two-suiter, and asking North to show his best suit as he would if responding to a take-out double.

2. 3 N.T. Compare **10A**, No. 2, where you only answered a D.A.B. with 2 N.T. Never leave to partner what you are good enough to do yourself, so here bid 3 N.T.

3. No Bid East has used an Unusual No Trump bid asking West for his choice between the *minors*. You have been warned off bidding clubs, so pass and await developments.

12A.

1. ♠ K 10 8 6	2. ♠ K Q J 8 5 4	3. ♠ A K Q 10 7 4
♡ 6 5 3	♡ A	♡ 8 5
◇ Q 7	◇ 4	◇ A Q
♣ Q 10 8 3	♣ A K J 10 7	♣ K Q J

W.	N.	E.	S.	E.	S.	W.	N.	E.	S.	W.	N.
1♣	2NT	3♣	?	1◇	2◇	No	2♡	1◇	2◇	No	2♡
				No	?			No	?		

Answers: Bid (2 pts.) Reason (3 pts.)

1. 4♣ North's bid is the Unusual No Trump requesting your choice between the minor suits with a possible sacrifice contract in mind. Your preference for clubs is too strong for you to take the opportunity, provided by East's bid, to pass. If North wants to bid on, you can go along with him.

2. 3♠ This will show North that your interest is in the black suits, not hearts.

3. 2♠ Even if North has a complete bust you want him to keep open until a game contract is reached. He knows, however, that you were too strong for a jump bid of 2♠ on the first round and will show 4-card suits in ascending order and you will repeat spades.

12B.

1. ♠ K J 10 9 7	2. ♠ 8 5	3. ♠ 9 3 2
♡ A Q J 10 4	♡ A K Q 10 7 4	♡ 9 8 6 4
◇ —	◇ K Q J	◇ 8 7 6
♣ K Q 6	♣ A Q	♣ 5 4 3

E.	S.	W.	N.	E.	S.	W.	N.	E.	S.	W.	N.
1◇	2◇	No	2♠	1♣	2♣	No	2◇	1♠	No	2◇	2 NT
No	?			No	2♡	No	2♠	No	?		
				No	?						

Answers: Bid (2 pts.) Reason (3 pts.)

1. 4♠ Eureka! North has a four-card spade suit! Even if it's only 8-high there is a good chance for game, so bid it.

2. 3♡ Reading you for possibly a spade-heart two-suiter, North is showing preference for spades. Confirm your single-suited hand by a heart rebid. North will surely put you to 4♡.

3. 3♡ North has shown a desire to compete in one of the unbid suits, hearts or clubs. You have no option but to tell him which you prefer as East has not let you off the hook by rebidding.

Also in Unwin Paperbacks

BASIC ACOL
Ben Cohen and Rhoda Lederer

Basic Acol is quick, easy, brief and to the point. First published in 1962, it proved so popular that a new Unwin Paperback version was necessary. This fifth edition is corrected and up-dated. The number of summary tables is now 45 and these cover the whole field of Acol bidding, even if only in outline. It is difficult to learn a complete system from summary tables only, without the help of a teacher or full textbook, but for the learner particularly, a quick and handy book of reference is a 'must'. *Basic Acol* is planned to give you an easy way to revise anything you have been taught, or to provide the quick answer to any bidding problems which may arise. This new version includes all recent developments in the Acol system as well as setting out clearly, with examples, the fundamental principles on which the system is based.

ALL ABOUT ACOL
Ben Cohen and Rhoda Lederer

All About Acol is the complete guide to the Acol System, by far the most widely used system in Contract Bridge. It describes the fundamental principles and includes the new features and developments in modern bidding which fit into the basic framework.

Modern Contract Bridge bristles with new devices, gimmicks and conventions. *All About Acol* has the latest information in up-to-date Acol Bidding combined with clarity and simplicity. With the help of the book the reader can sit down with any Acol – playing partner and use it with the minimum of difficulty, and maximum of success. It is indeed All About Acol.

ABC of Contract Bridge
  Ben Cohen & Rhoda Lederer   £2.95 ☐
Aces and Places *Rixi Markus*   £2.50 ☐
All About Acol *Ben Cohen & Rhoda Lederer*   £2.95 ☐
Basic Acol *Ben Cohen & Rhoda Lederer*   £2.95 ☐
Best Bridge Hands *Rixi Markus*   £2.95 ☐
Bid Boldly, Play Safe *Rixi Markus*   £2.50 ☐
Bridge Table Tales *Rixi Markus*   £1.95 ☐
Instructions for the Defence
  Jeremy Flint & David Greenwood   £2.50 ☐
Learn Bridge with the Lederers
  Tony & Rhoda Lederer   £2.95 ☐
Master Bridge by Question and Answer
  Alan Truscott   £1.95 ☐
The Only Chance *Eric Jannersten*   £2.95 ☐
Why You Lose at Bridge *S J Simon*   £2.95 ☐
Your Lead Partner *Ben Cohen & Rhoda Lederer*   £1.95 ☐

All these books are available at your local bookshop or newsagent, or can be ordered direct by post. Just tick the titles you want and fill in the form below.

_____

Name ....
Address ....
....
....

Write to Unwin Cash Sales, PO Box 11, Falmouth, Cornwall TR10 9EN.

Please enclose remittance to the value of the cover price plus:

UK: 55p for the first book plus 22p for the second book, thereafter 14p for each additional book ordered to a maximum charge of £1.75.

BFPO and EIRE: 55p for the first book plus 22p for the second book and 14p for the next 7 books and thereafter 8p per book.

OVERSEAS: £1.00 for the first book plus 25p per copy for each additional book.

Unwin Paperbacks reserve the right to show new retail prices on covers, which may differ from those previously advertised in the text or elsewhere.

Postage rates are also subject to revision.